Deborah [signature]

Eph 2:10

***I Made the Rainbow* is a story of hope.** Deborah candidly and humorously shares from the canvas of her own heart everything from how to fashion an inviting, warm home atmosphere to the benefits of forgiveness and the assurance that God's love will heal our past hurts and pain. Her creative use of the colors of the rainbow vividly paints the picture of wholeness in every area of a woman's life. You will be inspired to breathe new life into your home and your relationships while adding value to yourself as you allow the light of His rainbow to shine through.

-Marilyn Weiher
Co-author, *The Home Experience*: *Making Your Home a Sanctuary of Love and a Haven of Peace*

Deborah Dutton is masterful at making your home feel like a home and making you feel at home in her home! The orbit of her home gives you a big hug and an implicit welcome upon entry. Deborah possesses the gift of making others feel great about their surroundings, which is a ministry of love within itself. The words she penned in this book are just an extension of what she practices and gives with so much love! You will appreciate the gift of authenticity she offers as she mentors you in this book.

-Arnita Willis Taylor, MSL
Founder of Eight Leadership Development Group

I Made the Rainbow is a beautifully crafted book that brings together the skill of interior design and the heart to help people grow in their walk with God. Deborah is a true spiritual mentor. Reading this book is like welcoming a professional interior designer into your home to decorate while you also receive valuable insight from a seasoned life coach. Deborah addresses practical aspects of life and also speaks directly to the heart of life's important issues.

She is honest and transparent and you will love going on the journey with her as you read!

-Aaron Wronko
Pastor of Member Services, Gateway Church

Deborah Dutton has written a beautifully woven book on interior decorating that goes much deeper than paint on a wall. She artfully ties together the various colors God gave us and makes spiritual applications that had me saying, "Wow, I never thought of that" over and over again. This is a must read for those wanting to understand, not just interior decorating, but how to change your life and those dwelling with you by the design of your home.

-Jeff Wickwire
Senior Pastor, Turning Point Church
Author, *Making It Right When You Feel Wronged*

Deborah's, "I made the Rainbow" is gracious, authentic, and empowering. She will inspire you to have a home that's not only lovely but a true reflection of what matters most to you and a haven for those you love. This book will challenge you to really dream about the home you wish to create and give you the action steps to make your dreams a reality.

-Amy Ford
President, Embrace Grace
Author, *A Bump in Life: True Stories of Hope & Courage During an Unplanned Pregnancy*

Deborah Dutton's book is a grace-filled approach to the heart and home for women both young and old. In her beautifully written book, *I Made the Rainbow,* Deborah offers a practical approach on how we can connect with our homes while beautifying them in the process. This book will change you!

–Nancy Houston, LPC
Author, *Love & Sex*

I MADE THE RAINBOW

A Fresh Design Perspective From The Heart To The Home

Deborah Dutton

Published in Roanoke, Texas by Clear Wind Publishing.

Unless otherwise noted, all Scripture quotations are taken from the New King James Version®. Copyright © 1982 by Thomas Nelson. Used by permission. All rights reserved.

Scripture quotations marked (AMP) are taken from the Amplified Bible, Copyright © 2015 by The Lockman Foundation. Used by permission.

Scripture quotations marked (NIV) are taken from the Holy Bible, New International Version®, NIV®. Copyright © 1973, 1978, 1984, 2011 by Biblica, Inc.™ Used by permission of Zondervan. All rights reserved worldwide. www.zondervan.com The "NIV" and "New International Version" are trademarks registered in the United States Patent and Trademark Office by Biblica, Inc.™

Scripture quotations marked (NLT) are taken from the Holy Bible, New Living Translation, copyright ©1996, 2004, 2015 by Tyndale House Foundation. Used by permission of Tyndale House Publishers, Inc., Carol Stream, Illinois 60188. All rights reserved.

Scripture quotations marked MSG are taken from *THE MESSAGE*, copyright © 1993, 1994, 1995, 1996, 2000, 2001, 2002 by Eugene H. Peterson. Used by permission of NavPress. All rights reserved. Represented by Tyndale House Publishers, Inc.

Scripture quotations from the COMMON ENGLISH BIBLE. © Copyright 2011 COMMON ENGLISH BIBLE. All rights reserved. Used by permission.

Cover Image by Rolando Diaz.

Graphic Design by Zongquan Du.

Some names, places, and identifying details with regard to stories in this book have been changed to help protect the privacy of individuals who may have been involved or had similar experiences.

First Edition

18 19 20 21 22 – 9 8 7 6 5 4 3 2 1

Printed in the United States of America

CONTENTS

Dedicated To My Dear Friend, Jan Greenwood.

Thank you for your encouragement and for inspiring me to write this book.

"Words spoken at the right time are like golden apples in a silver basket." Proverbs 25:11 (CEB)

FORWARD

Home and family are so important to many of us. I personally long to experience family life in a home that is full of both peace and beauty. I want friends and family to enjoy coming through our front door, linger at our kitchen table or even spend the night as a treasured guest.

In my heart, I know the environment I want to create. Yet often I am disappointed in my own ability to fashion and maintain a home environment that accomplishes my dreams. I get caught up in what is lacking or "not perfect" and find myself dissatisfied and frustrated with the end result. It's like I can't quite accomplish what I can envision. It's easy to be overwhelmed and under inspired in regard to our home.

For many of us home is a place that reminds us of what we are not, what we don't have, or maybe even of some experience we would like to forget.

It could be as simple as the big pile of laundry or dirty dishes that are never really done. Maybe it's a relationship that is continually stressed. Or maybe it's just the mean old spirit of comparison that makes us long for what we don't have while we focus on what others do have. So how do we overcome these kinds of obstacles?

Many young women turn to the modern-day miracle called Pinterest—a visual search engine that every DIY-er uses to find inspiration. Some of us who are a little older still turn to our favorite magazines like *Architectural Digest, Home Beautiful* or *Good Housekeeping,* and if we can, we often hire an interior designer to help us bring it all together.

Most interior designers focus on the beauty of a space. They think of color, design and furniture placement from a perspective that is like a still-life painting. The beauty lies in perfect order and imaginary lifestyles. Rooms are like snap shots—perfect in a moment but not functional in real life.

Deb Dutton is an experienced interior designer whose perspective is so much more than that. Deb sees color, design and furniture as tools and expressions of our hearts that have the potential to come together in a palette that is both beautiful and functional; delightful and practical; inspiring and personal.

She is a colorful person. Not only is she statuesque with a great sense of style, but she has a personal flair that is reflected in her interior design, fashion and friendships. She tops all that off with a tender, wise heart and an infectious laugh. After all her years of experience in serving clients she's developed a language and lifestyle that reflect why and how she designs. All of this is then layered upon the foundation of her faith.

She creates beautiful places for real people to experience real life.

Deb and I became friends a few years ago on a mission trip to Belize. Deb has a certain kind of humor that breaks down walls and exposes hypocrisy. She called me out (in good fun) on a statement I made about the difference between a mission trip and a leadership trip. She made me giggle right away, but then she wouldn't let it go. We shared a room on that trip, and one night we literally stayed awake for hours, rolling in our beds and laughing hysterically like two teenage girls.

On that trip, I gained a friend who has a unique perspective on almost every topic. She also has a natural exuberance and an eye for beauty. While in Belize we visited a local small business owners' office. When we got back into our vehicle she told me she wished she had just one day to help them improve their store front presentation.

She would take what they already had, add a splash of paint, bring in a few plants and rearrange their furnishings to create some seating areas that were inviting. Then she'd frame some existing travel pictures from the local area and add some colorful art to make the whole place warm and inviting. In a moment, she was able to see how to completely transform their setting.

Not too long after we returned home, she came to my house for a walk through and consultation. She came into my home (bearing a gift) and within just a few moments began to see more clearly who I was and how I could better express myself within my own home through color, design and intentional simplicity. She began to mentor me in how to think about my home design in a different way and she made me feel empowered.

She will do the same for you.

In *I Made the Rainbow,* Deb shines as a mentor. She combines her professional experience, personal perspective and passionate faith to teach us how to do more than make our environments beautiful. She coaches us in how to make our homes a place of peace, love and beauty.

Just as God used the rainbow as a promise to mankind of hope and renewal, Deb uses the colors of the rainbow as a tool to help us look inside our own homes and hearts so that we can design a personal atmosphere that will reflect our hope for our family and friends. She not only teaches, mentors and coaches, she shares transparently. We are invited into her own journey of self-discovery and breakthrough in her marriage, parenting and personal faith. She helps us unmask the hidden experiences, misconceptions and even lies that keep us from experiencing our homes in a healthy way.

On top of all that, she will share some of her best design tips and tools. You'll learn about furniture placement, color selection, simplicity of design and how to use what you have. All of this will be laid out for you like a beautifully prepared dining table—each plate, dish, utensil and glass carefully and thoughtfully laid out for your pleasure.

I pray that as you dig into this amazing book you will ask yourself the tough questions; you will really dream about the kind of home you hope to create; and that you will go beyond reading and thinking to actually doing.

Here's to happy and fun designing!

-Jan Greenwood
Author of *Women at War*
Founder of Brave Strong Girl
Equip pastor at Gateway Church

RED

Chapter One

~HOME~

A POWER SOURCE

FOR HOPE

Do you remember what it was like when you first learned to color? In order to create the best coloring possible with clearly defined images, I was always taught to outline the area I was going to color first, and then color in the outlined spaces. This process created a neater look and allowed for the colors in my art to show clearly. Doing this at a young age, I discovered that if I didn't clearly define the boundaries of each area or space, my picture would look muddled and out of focus. However, by simply making outlines, I would create a clearer image.

It may seem like a simple analogy, but the truth is our lives and homes are similar to art on a canvas. By design, God has given each of us a "picture" to color. However, without clearly defined boundaries, our lives, like a painting, can end up looking muddled and unfocused. This is why purposeful design is so important, not only in art but also in life.

Design, according to Webster's dictionary means, "To plan and make decisions about something being built or created, to plan and make for a specific use or purpose" (Merriam Webster's Dictionary). This definition shows us how design is deliberate and in the same way, we should be deliberate about the lives and homes we are creating and *coloring.* There is an old proverb that says, "A wise woman builds her home" (Proverbs 14:1, NLT). In similar fashion, a wise woman builds her life through purposeful design.

Personally, when I look at the busy world we live in, I see stress, clutter, and the chaos of what we kindly refer to as "multitasking." Moms, grandmothers, sisters, and daughters are stressed and overloaded with the demands of life. So, while their lives might be busy and even fulfilling at times, without a clearly defined design, their values and vision can get blurred. Have you ever felt this way or noticed it happening in the life of someone around you?

Tragically, the results of a busy and overburdened life often lead to boredom and discontentment. But the good news is, life doesn't have to be this way, and if we will only stop for a moment, setting all distraction aside to take inventory of our lives and the path we are on, the results will be dramatic—shaping our future in a positive way.

Do you want to add more color, definition, and design to your life? I know I do, and when I design a home, I start by first understanding the life of the person I am designing for. Why? Because it is essential to invest time and commitment to the journey of discovery in order to better understand ourselves, define who we are, and define where we are going. Once this is accomplished, we will become empowered to add more balance, design, and color to our lives, our homes, and our world.

> *Without clearly defined boundaries, our lives, like a painting, can end up looking muddled and unfocused.*

Within the midst of this journey of discovery, it will also be important to stop and set aside time to ponder what we're learning. In the Psalms, King David often wrote, "Selah," which means, "to pause and calmly think of this." So, during these "Selah" moments, I may sometimes ask you to stop and get a cup of coffee or your favorite cup of tea in order to give space for you to pause and reflect upon what you're reading.

There will be places where I might say, "*Pause and ponder*," and this means it's a time for you to be still and really think about your life and the *design* you want to define for yourself and your home. I love this expression because it reflects the idea of slowly thinking or processing a thought—a type of wonderment is involved. But we first must be willing to prioritize our time in new, colorful and purposeful ways for positive change to happen.

Rainbow's Red

Whenever I think about design, color is one of the first things that comes to mind. Colors are essential, and the rainbow is where God's color palette first began. And the color red is what I believe to be the most important of all colors. It has the highest arc of the rainbow and the longest wavelength or, as I like to say, makes the most lasting impact, which is what our homes are created to do as well.

Studies suggest the color red even stimulates energy and may increase blood pressure, respiration, and heart rate, truly connecting red with the "heart" of the home. The psychology of color suggests that the color red makes people hungry. Red attracts attention, excites and energizes people, while also increasing the heart rate.

The color red encourages action and invokes feelings of confidence, while providing a sense of safety, which is what we all desire our homes to do. In many languages and cultures, red also represents beauty. For the Chinese, the color red symbolizes fire, and home is where we symbolically (if not literally) keep the home fires burning.

The truth is that in all societies, color represents various ideas and feelings. I've recognized this to be true in my life. And it's the reason that the color red represents so much that is key to purposeful design. It's a power color that stimulates and signifies passion and energy. For me, red truly is the one color that best represents the home.

Heart for Home

Where is your heart in relation to your home? Personally, I grew up in a stressful home, one that did not possess emotional wholeness. My home had it all—good times, bad times, and abusive times. Maybe you can relate to this. Perhaps your childhood home was a place of abuse and neglect.

In contrast, maybe you grew up in a home of complete perfection, where the mission of each day was to make sure everything was in order and spotless. This was the case in my husband's home. Dirty towels never touched the ground, and the floors were so pristine you would have felt safe eating off of them—though this was not encouraged!

Truly, the home encompasses numerous reflections and feelings, both positive and negative. But I think we can both agree that no matter where we currently find ourselves, or the season of life we may be in, we all want our homes to be a place where our hearts will be safe and find peace and solitude. Yet maybe you're wondering, "What do our hearts have to do with design?" And, in response, I would venture to say everything. All master designers begin with a plan in mind. For us, this plan begins in our hearts because that is truly what our homes reflect.

God has a divine plan and design for every person on the earth. Jeremiah 29:11 says, "For I know the plans I have for you," says the lord. "They are plans for good and not for disaster, to give you a future and a hope" (NLT). So, no matter what you may have experienced in your past, your home and your future can be full of hope. You may or may not feel like your present home is where your heart is, but you can change that. Not only are you the catalyst for your transformation, you can directly influence the formation of the hearts currently in your home: children, husbands, roommates, sisters, brothers, and mothers. You can make your home all it can be today.

Yet, if we allow it, our past homes can also limit us, hindering our success in life. However, it does not have to be this way. It is crucial that we separate our current home from any dysfunction we may have experienced in our youth. But, in order to have personal and emotional wholeness, we must allow God to define us and to define our current home through His plan of peace and hope. Jesus said, "The thief comes only to steal and kill and destroy. I came that they may have life and have it abundantly" (John 10:10 ESV).

No matter what your past, God has an abundant future for you and that includes your home as well as your heart! Maya Angelou once wrote, "The ache for home lives in all of us. The safe place where we can go as we are and not be questioned." In other words, we all have a God-given ache to create a home and to nurture the hearts within.

Pause and Ponder

In as few words as possible, answer the following questions.
1. Growing up, what was home for you?
2. What did home feel like?
3. What did home smell like?
4. What did home sound like and what were the words spoken there?

If the images and reflections are negative from your past, I want to encourage you to ask God to heal you in the specific areas you've been hurt and to help your current home become a new place—not defined by your past. After doing that, ask yourself:

1. What is home for me today?
2. What does it feel like?
3. What does it smell like?
4. How does it sound?
5. Is the home of my past playing a role in my home today (either positively or negatively)?

Friend, no matter what your answers to those questions might be, you can change your home and receive the grace you need from God to make it a better place—a place where hearts are formed by hope and peace.

"There's No Place like Home, There's No Place like Home."
— L. Frank Baum, *The Wizard of OZ*

In the late 1800's, there was a wealthy couple called to the mission field. They sold all they had and left for Central America. Upon arrival, their situation changed drastically. Their funds were stolen, and a promised position was lost. With their income gone, they lived day-to-day, barely able to provide food for their table. The husband was tempted to become bitter, feeling as though he had disappointed his dear wife. They moved into a rural hut belonging to one of their friends. It was completely unlike the mansion they had once enjoyed. The husband sank deeper into despair.

We all have a God-given ache to create a home and to nurture the hearts within.

One day after arriving home, rather than finding his wife pining-away over what they didn't have and how things used to be, the sweet aromas of freshly cooked stew and warm bread greeted him. Sweet humming flowed from the window and, as he opened the door, his wife rushed into his arms. She was smiling and happy to see him. He was in wonderment as he looked around, seeing the hut filled with wild flowers from the field and the smell of a fruit pie baking in the oven. There were touches of bright fabric on the windows and the space, though small, felt clean, and fresh.

What was the difference? The wife did not let her hut define her. Rather, she defined her *home*. I share this story with you because, as women, we have a powerful choice to make. And, with wisdom, we can define our homes no matter the obstacles—just like the assertive wife in this story. Let's get started.

Canvas by Design

I Made the Rainbow was birthed out of my desire to see women experiencing all God designed for their homes, lives, and families to be. This is why, using the colors of the rainbow, we will take a step-by-step journey that will help you to shape and design your home, as well as your life, into all that God created it to be.

I desire to paint for you a picture of *hope* for your home. But before we continue, let me ask you: How do you feel when you read or hear the word *hope*? Does it seem out of reach, like a distant dream, unobtainable? The good news is that there is hope, and it is available for you today.

Let's take some time to ***pause and ponder***. For the following questions, I encourage you to dream and use your five senses as you answer.

1. What do you hope your home looks like?
2. What do you hope your home smells like?
3. What do you hope your home feels like?
4. What do you hope your home sounds like?
5. What color is your home (not based on trend)?
6. Think of two words you hope your home speaks. For example, do you hope your home speaks of happiness, peace, elegance, or charm? Do you desire it to be simple and comfortable? Modern and fun?

Have fun with these questions and take your time finding the right words to describe your space. Then continue to reflect and dream as you answer the following questions.

1. How many do you hope will live in your home?
2. Are there velvets, furry pillows, rich woods, or flat stones?
3. What might be cooking on the stove right now in your kitchen?
4. How does your table look after you set it with loving

care? Do you feel a sense of satisfaction?

5. What music is playing right now? What do you hope the home tones will be?

I want you to write this dream down and hold onto this image of hope in your mind. This vision will become the blueprint that shapes your home as we go through your rainbow design.

Defining Hope for the Home

When I was nine years old, my family moved from Lake Jackson, Texas, to a family farm in Rushville, Ohio. I was at the end of the third grade and ready to make this new place my own. It happened that on this farm there was a corn crib, a type of granary used to store harvested corn. These small, cabin-like structures made from wood, typically had one-inch slats in the walls to allow the air to circulate in order to dry out the corn for feed. This rustic space quickly became my little playhouse.

Living on the farm, I discovered there were plenty of materials to design and decorate my little home, but the best decor came from our rather *lifeless* neighbors. You see, we lived right next to a cemetery and the flowers were often plastic roses in numerous colors. Eventually, these flowers would make their way to the cemetery's dump, until I collected them. I would crawl under the barbwire fence that separated our properties and sometimes I even got stuck on the wire. What a sight I must have been!

I remember the smell of the wild mint that grew on the farm (to this day when I smell mint I think of my farm days). The roses were on a wire stem and I would weave them perfectly into the little one-inch openings of the corn crib. I worked hard to turn my humble home into a show place. I didn't even play in it for fear I would mess-it up. But I share this because we all have the opportunity to define our homes, whether a mansion or a corn crib. Our *perspectives* alone limit us.

Is your home a shelter with four walls and a roof? Home could be as simple as a tent or maybe even have wheels! How many places have you lived in and called home over the course of your life? Statistically, the average American will move 12 times during their life. And for me, personally, I have lived in 18 different homes, four of which were on the same farm. However, I now have the joy of living in a home that I truly enjoy. And so can you!

Making Home Your Mission

As I just mentioned, growing up, my family moved a lot. On one auspicious occasion, we even lived above my mom's health food store. I was 12 at the time and I inherited the old cooler room as my bedroom. Again, perspective is everything. So, rather than feeling sorry for myself, I set out to design my space and make it my own. Because of this, that room became the birthplace of my designing career. My mom gave me complete freedom and I took it. I tie-dyed my window treatments and bedding. Then, using magazines, I installed artwork with toothpicks onto the Styrofoam walls. I wish I had a photo of it today—such a laugh! But this experience started my dream and desire for the art of purposeful design.

As women, as matriarch, we are the ones who define our homes, whatever form or shape they might be. You define home for you. So, what do you hope happens in your home? Growing, learning, healing, loving, fun? Proverbs 13:12 says, "Hope deferred makes the heart sick, but a dream fulfilled is a tree of life" (NLT).

If your home had a feeling, what would that feeling be today? How do you feel when you step through your door? Do you inhale a deep breath, grateful it feels so good to be home, or do you feel burdened and overwhelmed? Is the workload of your home out of control with dishes unwashed, closets a mess, and laundry piled high? Does your home feel miss-managed? Do you want to run for the door and bolt it?

Pause and Ponder

Find a comfy place to sit and get out your journal. I know it may seem challenging right now to see your home today with fresh eyes, but I want you to write a mission statement, which is simply a "statement of purpose." This will serve as the framework for how we will formulate together the strategy for achieving the home you desire. It will guide you, serving as a filter to separate what is important from what is not.

Mission Statement:

I want a home where _____, _____,

and _____ abide. Now say it

aloud—envision it—and let's make it happen!

RED

Chapter Two

FRESH PERSPECTIVE FOR

THE HOME

Design is all about heart perspective. Whereas some would say design is about current trends or what you feel might make others happy, truly, design is about creating beauty for your space and a style based on what you love.

In my design business, I meet people from all walks of life. And, as uniquely created humans, we all have different perspectives on life, relationships, and problems. But the way we communicate our perspectives to each other is either going to be life-giving or detrimental.

As I write this, I have been married for over 40 years. Sadly, I have not always valued or understood my husband's perspective, or his methods for doing things. I think the reason for this was that his way of seeing things was so different from mine. I didn't understand and, consequently, lacked perspective.

My Terry

I will never forget the first time I saw Terry Lynn. I was 19 at the time and playing saxophone in the church band for a Wednesday night church service. He was seated in the congregation and when I saw him, I could not believe my eyes! Terry was 24, and he was the best-looking man I had ever seen. My mouth flew open and I had to turn my head away to keep from staring. The thing is, he had seen me before at an Easter service, but I had never met him. I found myself looking at my mom and saying, "Is that Brenda's *little* nephew?"

Needless to say, it was difficult keeping my mind focused on the remainder of the service. And though Terry left early, I remember telling the Lord, "That is what I want!"

Well, it didn't take long for me to see that my prayer had been answered! I met Terry at the next service and the world faded away—leaving him alone in my vision. To this day, I describe it as love at first sight. We later talked on the phone and I don't know why, but I mentioned I liked the color yellow. The next church service, there he was seated in all his glory wearing a bright yellow suit.

Now, it's important to understand that I attended a very conservative church and most men wore dark suits with understated ties. He definitely had made a statement! And I thought it was sweet for him to try to impress me.

A true southern gentleman, Terry opened doors, gave flowers, and had a smooth southern accent (which our granddaughter declares is *Texan*). Here's the best part though—Terry was six feet six inches tall, and that meant I could wear any heels I wanted! This was important to me because I was five feet and nine inches tall, which was taller than any of the guys I had dated before when I wore heels.

> *Your perspective directly affects your attitude, and your attitude directly affects the tone of your home.*

All that to say, this dashing couple fell in love and two months later, Terry proposed. My dad was against long engagements and gave us only three weeks to plan the wedding. So, as we set off on our honeymoon, I remember thinking, "Who is this guy beside me? I'm with a stranger!" Our adventure had begun!

Yet from the very beginning of our journey together as a young couple, though we were very much in love, we lacked wisdom about defining our home and determining how it should feel.

I have always believed home has a spirit about it, either positive or negative. Because of this, the perspectives we have regarding those who are in our home directly influence the spirit of the home. For example, if I am viewing my husband through a negative perspective or interacting in a dishonoring way, my attitude will directly impact the spirit of our home.

In other words, your perspective directly affects your attitude, and your attitude directly affects the *tone* of your home.

Perspective and a Peculiar Problem

When I was in Kindergarten at Steven Foster Elementary in Jones Creek, Texas, I had a classmate named Gilbert. He was shy and never said much more than was required of him.

Now, Gilbert looked a little different from most children, not because he had large round eyes or because he was exceptionally tall and thin, it was that he had a large head. But, like most kindergarteners, we took daily naps by resting our heads on our desks for a designated time. (I'm sure this was more for the teacher than it was for us.) I was not one for naps. So, before our required "rest time" when we would line up at the water fountain for a drink, I would always fill my mouth up with water and not swallow it. I would wait until our heads were lying on our desks before letting the water slowly drain out of my mouth, forming a little "desk-puddle"—instant amusement, just add water.

One particular day, Gilbert provided more entertainment than I could ever create for myself. As I piddled with my puddle, I heard the teacher say in a very agitated tone, "Just hold still!" I looked up to see Gilbert, kneeling behind his chair with his head sticking through the wood slats—his face staring down where his behind should be.

Our teacher was trying to dislodge Gilbert's head, while Gilbert knelt whimpering. What a sight! She made it as far as his ears and then the yelling began. Tears were falling as poor Gilbert tried to cooperate with the teacher's efforts to free him. Finally, at her wits end, the teacher asked the school janitor to help extract Gilbert's head from the back of the chair. The school principal arrived, and he helped all the students exit the classroom. The janitor cut the chair open in order to free Gilbert. My kindergarten class was lined up and allowed to return as a new chair was brought in.

When the school day ended, my teacher looked at Gilbert and asked, "How did you get your head stuck in the chair in the first place?" No one had thought to ask him this question until that moment. Thinking to show her rather than tell her, Gilbert looked right at the teacher, sat up on his knees and slid his feet through the back of the opening in the chair. His entire body followed through, and there he was with his head lying on his seat all over again. The janitor could have freed poor Gilbert by simply sliding his thin, little body back through the chair, rather than slicing the chair open.

You see, so many things in life—whether a perceived problem or possible opportunity—lead back to the importance of perspective. And our homes are no different!

Pause and Ponder

Let's take some time to *pause and ponder*. These questions may feel challenging, but they are important for your life canvas.

1. Is there an atmosphere of honor and encouragement in your home?
2. Is there a positive perspective in your home, one that empowers you to love one another? If not, do you find there is discord, anger, and strife in your home? If you answered yes to this question, please don't feel shame or guilt. Today, God is here to empower you to change and give you hope! By simply thinking new thoughts about your home and those who live there, you can begin to improve the atmosphere of your home.

Think Red

Now, I can imagine you might be wondering, "How do I get the right perspective?" Well, we can start by making sure our thoughts and meditations are life giving. Philippians 4:8–9 says, "Summing it all up, friends, I'd say you'll do best by filling your minds and meditating on things true, noble, reputable, authentic, compelling, gracious—the best, not the worst; the beautiful, not the ugly; things to praise, not things to curse. Put into practice what you learned from me, what you heard and saw and realized. Do that, and God, who makes everything work together, will work you into his most excellent harmonies" (MSG).

I love that verse because it reveals the key to keeping the right perspective for our homes. Sadly, however, it was one that took my husband and me many years to learn, and even more to put into practice.

If Walls Could Talk

I'm sure you would agree that many houses might appear to be great homes. They look nice on the outside and you might even see parents playing with their children in the front yard. But what's on the outside doesn't always reflect what is truly the case within. And if the walls of my house could talk, they would tell a story of past emotional and verbal abuse—where fussing and fighting were considered normal. They would tell you of the dishonor and name-calling that took place. Yet when we stepped outside our home, with my little girls dressed in matching socks and hair bows, and me and Terry acting lovingly toward each other, no one would have suspected the difficulties within our home.

Unfortunately, my husband and I were allowing our past homes to define our present home. And it simply was not working. Pride lies to the family in this home saying, "There is no hope. How could your home be any different from the home you grew-up in?" And, as a result, shame and secrecy further hinder change from ever happening. Perhaps you're even thinking now, "If someone knew the truth of what's happening in my home, it would crush me."

Shame tries to shroud us in darkness, causing our homes to be ineffectual "power-sources" for our loved ones and us. For the person causing the pain or abuse, shame keeps them from getting help and healing. But for the one *receiving* the abuse, shame keeps them from change.

In my case, the events of verbal abuse were mostly on special occasions and my husband was always sorry for his behavior later. Yet unbeknownst to me, the hurtful words were building a wall around my heart to the point I no longer saw his words as abuse, until I really got a wake-up call one anniversary when a waiter quietly stood behind my husband and silently asked me if he could call for help.

I had thought no one could hear my husband's words or see my pain. I was wrong. Like many women, I thought I could handle the abuse and if I only did more or tried harder, maybe the abuse would stop and go away. But that was not the reality.

Though Terry and I always had love, passion and remained faithful to one another, the truth is, there were times of separation. And even a time when Terry asked me for a divorce.

The turning point for us came during a grave illness Terry went through. During this season, we began to understand for the first time how blessed we really were to have each other. Yet, though I wish I could say we found a magic, marriage wand and waved it over our family, the healing process wasn't that simple.

For years, Terry did not value me. And for years, I did not honor him. But not only did I not feel valued by my husband, I also didn't value myself. We had little in common and could not agree on much. Worse, we let each other know it too. We were too busy "fighting it out" to declare peace and love over our home. And, because of this, my poor girls were not raised in the red sphere of the rainbow, where home is the power source that can recharge their little hearts.

Our journey to a healthy marriage and home began with our commitment to one another—a commitment that was not about how we felt at the time. And it required a lot of work, involving marriage events, books, seminars, counseling, and much prayer. To this day, my two favorite marriage books are *Marriage on the Rock* by Jimmy Evans and *Keep Your Love On,* by Danny Silk. Both of these authors are able to teach about connection in marriage in a way that is easy to understand.

The first time Terry and I met with a counselor, I remember telling her, "I can't make him happy!" She looked at me and said, "You're not supposed to make him happy. Only God and the peace that Jesus brings can do that!" I was shocked! I found myself thinking that all my efforts to try harder, all my self-doubt and romantic dinners were for nothing.

Sadly, I am not writing all of this from a place of, "Here is how we did it! You can do it too!" I am writing as a woman who desires greatly to share with other women how they can learn from my mistakes and victories and make their home the *red* power source God designed it to be.

By God's grace, I faced my truth by "drawing a line in the sand" and today is different. My home is now the *red* zone, where little hearts feel love and peace. I am now blessed by the grace and healing that covers my marriage and my heart. It has been a long journey with plenty of bumps and setbacks. Even in seasons when I didn't think our family would survive, my husband and I never gave up on our home or our marriage. I just had to learn to value myself and ask for help.

Now, some habits will never change. I often still drive the long way to get to places even if there's a shortcut available, and he still needs a beverage for the road even if we are just going across the street. But we have value, love, and understanding for each other. We may be different, but we are one team. So, I want to encourage you that if there is abuse in your home, seek help now. Don't wait, thinking you can handle it on your own. Make your home a safe zone.

Pause and Ponder

It's time to outline your heart with red. Make yourself a cup of tea or some yummy coffee and allow God to help you face what is *your* truth. Sit quietly for a while. Ask your walls to talk, sounds crazy, but listen—just listen. If you don't like what you're hearing, get a new perspective by asking God for wisdom. Ask Him to heal your home and heal the hearts within.

Write down what you feel God is saying to you and what His dream is for your home. Write down what you would like the tone of your home to sound like. Finally, ask God for the strength and grace to make new memories within your walls.

RED

Chapter Three

THE BLESSING

One day, I attended the house blessing of my dear friend, Carol, and her husband, Buddy. They had recently moved and invited family and friends over to pray a blessing over their lovely new home. Carol and Buddy did this because they knew that they, as well as the people around them, had the power to speak a blessing over their home through their words.

Proverbs 18:21 says, "Words kill, words give life; they're either poison or fruit—you choose" (MSG). We have a great responsibility from God to speak blessings over our homes and over those who live there.

For Buddy and Carol, they also have a Hebrew blessing called a Mezuzah that hangs by their door to remind them consistently to speak blessing. The Mezuzah contains a verse from Deuteronomy 6:4–9 written on one side of a piece of paper. On the other side is written Shaddai, which is one of the names of God and means, "The All Sufficient God." This paper is folded, placed inside a small box, and fastened to the door-post. The Mezuzah is a wonderful visual that reminds family members, as they come in and out, to continually speak blessings over their home and family.

Perhaps you want to have a home blessing. If so, I encourage you to call some family and friends who care about your home and ask them to walk through it and pray blessings. If you don't know what to speak, simply read Deuteronomy 6:4–9, as well as Numbers 6:24–26 (MSG), "God bless you and keep you, God smile on you and gift you, God look you full in the face and make you prosper." God loves you and your family, and He wants you to declare words of peace and love over your home because your words are powerful!

Shabbat

I love the movie *Fiddler on the Roof*. In one of the scenes, the father and mother sing a blessing over their children. What a great idea—though you don't have to sing if you don't want to! When my husband and I moved into our first home, I was only concerned with how our home looked (where to hang art and how many new pieces of furniture I could afford). I was viewing our home similarly to how I viewed my little corn crib house—all staged, never messed up by someone actually living there.

Yet there is so much more to purposefully designing your home than just how it looks. As the woman of the house, you play an essential role in ushering in God's blessing for your home. And the Biblical tradition of the Sabbath, which the Jewish culture refers to as Shabbat, is a powerful aspect of this. It begins every Friday evening at sundown when the woman of the house lights two candles. One candle stands for "Zakhor," which means to remember. The other candle stands for "Shamor," which means to keep or guard.

After lighting the candles, the mother waives her hands over the flames three times, which symbolically welcomes in the Sabbath. Then, covering her eyes, prays: "Blessed are You, LORD our God, King of the universe, who sanctified us with His commandments and commanded us to kindle the Sabbath candles." She might even offer a silent or verbal blessing on behalf of her husband and children after praying this prayer.

I share this wonderful Shabbat process with you because it is a wonderful visual picture of how vital you are to your family and to the success of your home—making it a red source of hope. As the matriarchs of our homes, we must remember to keep and guard the spirit of our home. And in the same way the Jewish mother will welcome in the Sabbath, so can you welcome in the spirit of hope and rest in your home, declaring peace and blessing over your family and all who are with you.

Pause and Ponder

Take some time to write a statement or prayer to inspire the spirit you hope to have in your home. Let this hope for change cover your heart. Make it a declaration over your home, even saying it aloud several times a day. Maybe you can write it down on a pretty piece of paper and frame it—hanging it in a place where you will see it and remember often to speak words of God's favor. The "ears" in your walls will hear a new song and the spirit of your home will begin to change as you speak blessings. Your perspective will also shift as you give God room to move in your home as you speak words of life!

A Ketchup Explosion

My mother-in-law was a great cook, however, when Terry and I first married, I was lacking in the culinary department. I could cook, but not my husband's favorites and certainly not like his mama. We often went to Terry's mother's home for dinner, so she could make "Bubbies" favorite foods.

One time, I was helping to clear the table after one of Dodo's dinners, and I set the ketchup in the refrigerator. Quickly, my mother-in-law exclaimed, "Oh, no, I keep the ketchup bottle in the cabinet. I like it warm and my mama always kept it in the cabinet." I gave in and that was the end of it.

A few weeks later, we arrived at Terry's parent's home, with appetites ready for her amazing chicken-fried steak. We blessed the food and Terry's father, Eugene, excused himself to go to the restroom. Ketchup always added to the flavor of the chicken-fried steak, and as Terry opened the glass ketchup bottle, it sounded like a shotgun went off, as the metal cap shot straight into Terry's eye. He quickly pressed his hand against his socket as blood began to flow down his cheek. His poor mother jumped up and began running up and down the hall yelling, "Eugene, Eugene! Get off the pot! Terry put his eye out with the ketchup bottle! Eugene, Eugene! Terry put his eye out with the ketchup bottle!" I quickly retrieved an ice pack and pried his hand away from his face. Thankfully, he only had a small eighth-inch cut just above his eye.

After this experience, we realized that when ketchup doesn't remain in a cold environment like the fridge, it can ferment and cause an "explosion" when opened. So, let's just say the ketchup bottle was kept in a new place after that—the fridge!

Hope for Order

Have you ever heard the expression, "A place for everything and everything in its place?" I don't know who came up with this simple phrase, but for some of us (myself included), it is just not that simple!

My husband and I now enjoy living in a townhome. It's simple to keep up. But everything in its place did not come easy for me. In the past, my discontent, designer heart would get the better of me and I would think to myself, "I can design this space to look better!" So, I would go through endless options in my head.

Maybe I needed new art for the walls or fresh pillows for the sofa. Maybe, if I moved this piece of furniture over there and painted this wall a different color, the room would look better. You get the picture!

I was never satisfied. I would tear up my house and put it back together again in different ways only to change it again soon after. I realize now all this maneuvering was just a distraction. As long as I was staging my playhouse, I did not have to live in it.

In other words, my idea of order was to continually redo everything. Many times, my poor husband would leave for work and come home to a complete designer war zone. Furniture moved, bedding piled high, paint buckets sitting out, and ladders mid-room. What a mess! On one such occasion, Terry had gone to work and at that time, faux finishes were the buzz. I decided to faux the kitchen a camo-green with a teal glaze. I thought this would look great with my cream cabinets and fruit-printed window treatments.

Terry returned home from work to complete chaos. The walls were army green, the room was littered with ladders and paint buckets, dinner was not made, and I was exhausted! He just stared at me and said, "Well, everything you have done in the past has turned out great, but I have my doubts about this time."

Thank goodness, Terry knew how to paint. He has bailed me out of more messes than I can count. I mainly selected my renovation débuts when company was coming—in order to maximize the stress! I always had great intentions, but never planned for how long the project would actually take.

Now, there must be order and organization for a home to be all it was designed to be. But many of us are overwhelmed and have no idea where to start. If this is an area of weakness for you (as it is for me), it can be helpful to read as many books on this topic as you can until one speaks to you. 2 Timothy 2:15 says, "Study to show thyself approved unto God, a workman that needs not to be ashamed, rightly dividing the word of truth" (KJV). Our homes should serve us, not the other way around. And, through study and diligence, we can learn how to live in a home of hope and order.

Custom-Made Organization

Faith, one of my best friends, was a professional organizer. I always loved going to her home because it was neat and tidy. Her closets brought me to tears. The clothes would be hung perfectly, they were always color-coded and looked straight out of a magazine photoshoot.

> *There must be order and organization for a home to be all it was designed to be.*

I would love to be like that but, for some reason, I didn't receive her genetic organization gifting. For years, in my business as a professional designer, I would have fabric samples piled high on my sofa, another client's window treatment designs stacked on my coffee table, and misplaced paint swatches hidden in forgotten crevices. I longed for my office to look like other offices, but I was lost.

Eventually, I succeeded in making my office "look good," but it was not "functionally good" for my needs. That's when I discovered large, clear zip-file bags from the Container Store. I was able to store each client's design samples and drawings in these easy-to-use bags. This was organization made simple and it worked for my personality.

Next, I designated a clipboard for each client, enabling me to keep important documents, receipts, and invoices in an organized place. This method of organization has served me well, especially since I often needed to grab and go.

Here's why I share all of that with you: when it comes to finding systems for your home or office, it does not have to be a "one-size-fits-all" approach. Discover what works for you. You may have to "tweak" your systems as you go, but eventually you will find an approach to organization that empowers you and brings peace to your home.

Hope for the Space

When approaching the topic of organization, it is important to have a realistic perspective. For example, if you live in a small apartment, having five sets of dishes is not living within your reality. Living within your means does not just apply to money, it also applies to space.

Personally, I enjoy planning what I call a "nesting-day" where the plan for the day is bringing order to my home (more on this topic later). If the thought of clearing clutter overwhelms you, try this simple plan: block out 15 minutes a day to address an area of need in your home. Start at your entry and work your way forward. Do so as fast as you can, keeping it to 15 minutes, so you will be more likely to do it again the following day. Celebrate little victories and be content with small steps of improvement. Your house didn't become disheveled in one day, so do not expect it to look like a magazine overnight. Remember, you are living in your home too, and, where there is "life," there will always be a little bit of a mess!

Raising three girls, I discovered what worked best for me regarding how to keep the home running smoothly. With having four girls under the same roof (including myself), you would think someone had to share a shoe size. But the four of us had sizes of eight, nine, ten, and eleven (I was the eleven). And, as you can imagine, the under-garments were an organizational nightmare!

After completing the laundry, I would spend hours trying to figure out what went to Terah's room and what went to Taneia's room (Tessa's clothes were easy because she was the smallest). Eventually, I designed a plan and gave each girl their own laundry basket, assigning them a specific laundry day. Thankfully, I never mixed their clothes again. Another idea that also worked well in our home was the rule that no clean laundry could remain in the laundry room. The laundry came out of the dryer and into the rooms (this kept the piles down). I also taught my girls how to do their own laundry, which was an excellent way to teach them responsibility.

Another key characteristic of our home was that my girls shared a bathroom. Because of this, I gave them each their own bath bucket for their personal essentials and monogramed towels. Next, I placed a lighted makeup mirror in each room for their beauty needs—this eliminated any stress over the bathroom time.

The perspective here is simple: find a system that works well for the top three issues in your space and do it! Look at the areas of stress in your home and formulate a plan that works for you. You may have to try a few ideas, but eventually you will discover your organizational style. Sometimes it can even be helpful to invite a friend over who is gifted in this area and ask them for some tips. Just like hiring a designer, an organizer can help you see the space in a new light.

Systems work best when everyone is helping with ideas, so get the whole family involved. It is amazing how much peace will fill your heart and home when you begin to get things in order. Today, start by taking just one-step in the right direction.

Three Key Pieces

Now that we have defined our home, let's talk furniture. We all want our homes to be red powerhouses, providing energy for our loved ones, and furniture plays an essential role.

When it comes to furniture, comfort and quality are key ingredients. We will discuss many important furniture pieces throughout this book, but for now, I am going to focus on the bedroom. The average American sleeps eight to nine hours a night. Over the course of a year, these numbers add up to approximately 125 days spent sleeping! But are you getting the kind of sleep and rest that leaves you feeling energized and ready to face each new day?

A good mattress is vital for experiencing a restful night's sleep; however, a good bed also needs to be aesthetically pleasing. We should love the feeling we get when we lay our heads on our pillows. Good cotton sheets, with a thread count of at least 300, make a significant improvement to the overall quality of our bed's feel. And your pillows should not be worn or odorous. While it may take a little research, getting the right mattress will further the completion of creating a bed that invites you to sleep on it.

There are many mattresses to choose from and the pricing as well as the materials used may be "over-the-top." For example, some beds are made from horsehair, while others are made from seaweed with prices rising as high as $100,000.00! I don't know that I would sleep well on this type of a mattress, but the point here is that with all the options available, there is no excuse for not having a comfortable bed to fall into at night.

The sofa is next in line as an essential part of a functional and beautiful home. When Terry and I were first married, we inherited a lovely sofa with a green, orange, and yellow plaid fabric. It had classic lines and was extra-long. My tall husband loved this sofa because he could completely stretch out on it. I knew little about sofas and, being put off by the colors, I completely overlooked the quality of the sofa and how well it was made. I didn't realize the best sofas have a hardwood frame for proper support and are eight-way hand-tied. (Eight-way hand-tied is the highest quality of furniture and provides stability within the sofa that keeps the springs from shifting. The sofa will remain comfortable for longer.)

I was tired of looking at green, orange, and yellow plaid, and I could not wait to get rid of this hand-me-down! Yet when the blessed day came, I unknowingly purchased an inferior sofa. The colors were right; but if I knew then what I know now, I would have kept the quality sofa I had inherited and simply reupholstered it.

> *"She has prepared her meat and mixed her wine; She has also set her table"*
> *Psalm 128:3 (NIV)*

Even now, you might have a treasure and not even know it. Reupholster sofas just have a classic, quality design.

Now, about color, solids are the best and by simply adding some colorful throw pillows and artwork, you can update the look of your space. Just be sure to spend some time sitting on the sofa before you purchase it. The average person will keep their sofa for approximately ten years and sometimes even longer if they are well made.

When it comes to fabric, it's important to consider what season of life you are in. For example, if you have young children in the home, you may want to consider a leather sofa as it's easy to clean and durable. But also keep in mind that leather can sometimes look cold, so consider mixing other furniture pieces like a fabric chair to soften the look. Truly, it's up to you regarding what style you prefer. (Tufted, with a simple back is my favorite sofa design.) Just remember, a neutral colored sofa in a soft fabric is always in style. Make the throw pillows pop with color and be sure it's a comfy place to relax.

Do you know what the most important piece of furniture is in your home? Here's a hint: it's so important that God had it in

His home and it was referred to as the tabernacle. But for us, the answer is the table.

Recently, I was blessed to travel on a mission trip where I noticed many of the homes had televisions and beds, but no tables. This grieved me because I knew a table could bless their homes and families in more ways than they realized. They just didn't understand how one of Jesus's last acts was to bring the most important people in his life to a table to enjoy a last meal before the cross.

In Italy, "Gioie della tavola" translated means, "The joys of the table," and this phrase is showcased in great works of Italian art throughout the ages—celebrating the evening meal. But a recent survey discovered that 40 percent of American families eat together less than three times a week, with ten percent of families never eating together at all. However, further studies reveal that having a meal together five times a week can reduce drug abuse and immorality amongst young people.

The Table: From a Palace to the Home

One of my favorite "table" stories is found in II Samuel 9:1–13. It is the story of Jonathan's son, Mephibosheth.

After the death of King Saul and his son Jonathan, David became King. After a short time had passed, David asked, "Is there still anyone who is left of the house of Saul, that I may show him kindness for Jonathan's sake?" (II Sam 9:1, NKJV). David discovered that Jonathan's now crippled son still lived, so he immediately invited him to sit at the king's table—his table...

"His name was Mephibosheth; he was Jonathan's son and Saul's grandson. When he came to King David, he bowed low to the ground in deep respect. David said, 'Greetings, Mephibosheth.' Mephibosheth replied, 'I am your servant.' 'Don't be afraid!' David said. 'I intend to show kindness to you because of my promise to your father, Jonathan. I will give you all the property that once belonged to your grandfather Saul, and you will eat here with me at the king's table!'...And from that time on, Mephibosheth ate regularly at David's table, like one of the king's own sons" (II Samuel 9:6–8, 11, NLT).

The table was a place of healing for Mephibosheth and, though it can seem basic, so many are missing the opportunity of health and wholeness that sitting around the table brings. Simply by preparing some food and gathering family and friends to eat a meal together, everything can change for the better. And if our home is to be a powerful place to recharge at the end of each day, this significant act shouldn't be missed.

Growing up, there was always a lot of stress and discipline around my family's table. I have memories of hardly being able to swallow my food because the tension was so high. But as an adult, I determined to make the table a fun, inviting, and elegant place in my home. I have three daughters and I think they would all agree one of their most memorable occasions took place one year when it was their father's birthday.

Sadly, he was very ill at the time. In fact, we weren't sure if he would survive. Terry weighed only 165 pounds and was in a lot of pain. For his birthday, I wanted to lighten the spirit in our home, so I made a chocolate cake and his favorite meal. I set the table with cloth napkins and my best china, arranging his presents beside the table. We all gathered to eat, but Terry couldn't eat much and said he needed to go rest. As he took his frail body to bed, my three sweet little girls and I sat in silence. No one wanted to ask if daddy would get well—the girls knew it wasn't good. There was a deep sadness, as is the case in many homes when a loved one is suffering, and it felt unbearable.

There we sat, food hardly touched, and a chocolate cake uneaten. Suddenly, I took my finger, dipped it into the frosting, and put it on my older daughter's nose. From there we all lost it— putting the cake on each other and laughing so hard. I ended up with a chocolate facial. It didn't even matter that my elegant dining room was being smeared with cake shrapnel. We laughed until we had tears. By God's grace, my husband regained his health and the season of sadness passed. Our table served us well that night.

Pause and Ponder

What was your table experience like growing up? Was there a table prepared for you each night? Are the memories of your family table positive or negative? When was the last time you had a meal at your table? Take time to look back at the vision statement you wrote. How can you organize your home to reflect your vision statement? What would your bed and sofa look like if they accurately reflected your vision? Finally, what would life around your table look like if it matched your vision?

Make the table a place for connection, not correction. And welcome in the blessing of red, embracing hope for your home today. I hope this helps you see clearly the new vision and mission for your home!

ORANGE

Chapter Four

DILIGENT DESIGN

**"Let the favor of the Lord our God be upon us, and
Establish the work of our hands upon us;
Yes, Establish the work of our hands!"
Psalm 90:17, ESV**

Colors are so powerful. They possess meaning, stimulate memories, cause feelings and create experiences. Because of this, it's important to make our homes a "red" power source. But now it's time to deliberately design our home by embracing the next color in the rainbow—orange.

The color orange represents the idea of thoughtful and diligent design in our homes and lives. It symbolizes determination, warmth, stimulation, and success. In early Native American culture, the color orange was a symbol of kinship, which I feel is appropriate as we intentionally design our home to foster relationships. It's a color that always uplifts and infuses warmth and confidence wherever it is seen. And, in the same way, I want to empower you to inject energy and fun into your home through purposeful, diligent design.

As I shared earlier, I was 12 when I realized my gift for design. My father had purchased what was referred to then as the old Kauffman farm, and an old Victorian mansion came with the property. Though it must have been beautiful in days gone by, it had come to a place of complete disrepair with peeling paint and boarded-over windows. Yet for a dreamer like me, the house was enchanting. I lived there in my mind and I knew the color and plan of each room. What a wonderful time for my developing my creativity and design sense.

When I turned fourteen, my parents built their dream home on this farm. I enjoyed watching the workers each day, until the day the painters came. I knew the paint color was completely wrong. I called my dad and told him he could not paint the walls that color!

Not wanting to be bothered, he said, "Then you pick it!" So, I did. And I went on to select all the light fixtures, counter tops, furniture, and window treatments. This design experience made an indelible impression on my life.

Whether you feel like you have a gift for decorating or not, designing your home is an obtainable goal. I'm passionate about design, but even more passionate for women to reach their full potential in their lives and in their homes. Since 1994, I have been an interior designer, and now I want to share tools for successfully designing your home. Through diligent design, you can create a home environment filled with harmony, joy, relaxation, and kinship.

Design is like a symphony. The music sounds best when your rooms sing in harmony; some elements can be louder, while others may sing softly. I like to think you can hear a different song in each room as long as they're in tune, and I desire for your home to be music to your eyes and heart.

"I will make your towers of sparkling rubies, your gates of shining gems, and your walls of precious stones."
Isaiah 54:12, NLT

God wants to allow His creativity and wisdom to shine so you can create beauty and worth in your space, making a home that sings. Because of this, keep in mind the mission statement you wrote for your home, though this journey is about more than the design of your home. It is a journey of renovating our lives and families.

Ecclesiastes 3:1–2 and 11 says, "TO EVERYTHING there is a season, and a time for every matter or purpose under heaven: A time to be born and a time to die, a time to plant and a time to pluck up what is planted...He has made everything beautiful in its time" (AMP, emphasis added). No matter what your present season, now is the time for you to embrace a new chapter of your life and to take new ground in your homes and families. Today, you can ask God to help you shape your home into a nurturing environment.

Do you ever think about what God's home looks like? Isaiah 40:22 says, "He spreads out the heavens like a curtain and makes His tent from them" (NLT). And Isaiah 66:1 reads, "This is what the Lord says, 'Heaven is my throne, and the earth is my footstool'" (NLT). Personally, I have sometimes wondered, "How would I decorate for Jehovah God?" Would I hang famous works of art from the ages? The possibilities would be infinite!

Through observation of nature, astronomy, or human composition, it is impossible to say God does not care greatly about design. God changes the earth's

> "Good seasons start with good beginnings."
>
> – Sparky Anderson

décor every three months and the color pallet is perfection. Across the world, at any given time, He creates a sunset or sunrise that's new every time!

While in Hawaii with my husband to renew our vows one year, I watched in awe each morning and evening as God, the Artist, unfolded His masterpieces. He painted for us the most glorious sunsets and sunrises we ever saw—such a gift. God is the ultimate designer and His designs are matchless. But we can design too, because He created us in His image!

It may be easy to assume plans for our lives or homes are insignificant, but the truth is just the opposite. God created the earth with intentional design, and He shares His designs with mankind. In fact, He placed it in our care. I can only imagine what my living room would look like, placed in the care of my grandchildren!

Consider how God gave Moses specific details for building the tabernacle. God was just as concerned with the design and details of the temple that He wanted King Solomon to build. Design matters to God. What about Noah who took one-hundred years to build the ark? What do you imagine the plans God gave for the ark may have looked like? God took great care in giving Noah a specific design for the ark, and in the same way, we should take care in how we design our home.

Jesus said, "Consider the lilies, how they grow: they neither toil nor spin; but I tell you not even Solomon in all his glory clothed himself like one of these" Luke 12:27 (NASB). Jesus declared how God clothes the grass in the field, which is alive today and gone tomorrow. If it's important to God to clothe the lilies and the fields, how much more as His daughters should we consider "clothing our homes" with beauty through design? We should take great care and have details in our living spaces.

By now, I know you are thinking a lot about your home and possibly your style. Maybe you have already made some changes for the better, even if the changes are as simple as making the bed in the morning. Whatever the change, I don't want this journey to overwhelm you. If making changes and working on a space right now feels too challenging, lay it aside for a more opportune time. It is okay to be patient with yourself and with the process of designing your space. The best results happen when you are ready. There needs to be a flow and a rhythm with design. So quiet yourself, lay aside any projects you are trying to multi-task and feel out the space you want to change. Allow yourself the freedom to dream of the possibilities each room offers. Let the changes around you start from within you!

Design and Emotions

One Christmas, my design services were a present for a client. Her husband was a builder and he was proud of their home, so he gave my design time to his wife and wished me luck. His wife had designed their great room around her grandmother's lovely china, which was teal with wine colored berries. She felt it would highlight the china if she combined teal and wine colors on the wall.

Now, I love to start a design project with something that inspires my clients, but teal and wine walls were not going to work! She was torn, not knowing how to feature the china, while also making the space her own. I decided we needed to go shopping. After visiting show room after show room, my client would tell me what she loved while turning to something completely different to say, "But this would work in my home."

Having lived in California, she loved designs with a touch of "Mission style" to them. But now, after marrying into a large Texas family, she felt confused regarding her personal style. We selected a rug and headed to lunch, where I shared with her what I had observed—she was not selecting things that "sang" to her. She was pensive and decided she needed to return the rug.

Later, we were able to design the room to her perfect taste and the china was still displayed, but in a way that showcased her unique style. Design is emotional and requires us to be honest about what we like and don't like. Keep in mind that rooms express feelings. They can either express warmth, charm, peace, or be overly cluttered and busy, which communicates stress and discord.

I love this saying by Emily Barnes, "When you make yourself at home, you surround yourself with the people you love, the objects you cherish, the memories that warm you, and the ideas that motivate you." Let this quote resonate with you. Create an environment that expresses all the beauty, creativity, and color of who God made you. Ask God to give you wisdom to reflect His beauty in the design of your home.

Philippians 4:6–7 says, "Don't fret or worry. Instead of worrying, pray. Let petitions and praises shape your worries into prayers, letting God know your concerns. Before you know it, a sense of God's wholeness, everything coming together for good, will come and settle you down. It's wonderful what happens when Christ displaces worry at the center of your life" (MSG). Allow God to unlock the unique colors inside of you, as you embrace diligent design and add the color of orange to your home!

Pause and Ponder

Grab a cup of tea or your favorite cup of coffee and value yourself enough to take the time to stop and reflect over everything you have just read. What is your heart saying to you? Diligent design takes great honesty, so ask yourself: when you open the door to your home, does the space draw you in? Is it singing to you and embracing you with a hug? Are you unable to define what the style is saying or who lives there? Is your sleeping area comfy and restful or is it pulling at you—full of to-dos with no peace? Whose personality lives in your space? Your mom, your friend, or someone unrelated to you? Does your space possess a past, present, and future, or is it only past? How are your rooms, touching your five senses: sight, smell, touch, sound, taste? Does your favorite color play a part in your design? Which parts of your room or your home brings you delight, joy and fun. Why?

Reflect upon the Master of design, our heavenly Father, and how He uses color. Most individuals love either blue or green. If you are one who loves blue, think about how God used blue and added white clouds with touches of orange kissed by a pink sunset. I believe God has secret designs hidden away in the ocean's depths the eye has never seen, and great stones buried deep in the ground no man could ever touch. I have secret designs in my home, things that have meaning and beauty to me and no one else, such as little trinkets inside a lovely box or a folded note tucked away in a drawer just for me.

Today, find something special, something precious, and tuck it in a secret place—a place that brings you joy and will make you smile! I have a blue glassfish on display, it brings a smile to my face and joy in my heart. There are times I even laugh when I see it. Don't forget to have fun making life more colorful around you. Write down in your journal how you can make your design dreams a reality today!

ORANGE

Chapter Five

KEEPING PACE

Many years ago, I had a client, a single woman, who wanted to have her master suite designed. Yet she had no idea where to begin, she didn't know what she liked, what her favorite colors were, or what design style she was looking for. Her home was a total blank canvas.

Now, the hardest client for me to work with is the client with no starting point or style preference. And this client couldn't even find a pillow she liked. So, I decided to go through her closet in order to get some impressions of what she might like, and, to my amazement, I discovered bold colors with gold buttons and loud, vivid prints. With this knowledge, I designed her room in an apricot color using gold and silver accents. The room turned out glorious, and she loved it.

I share this because it's essential you have a clear vision of the space you desire to live in. Take some time to sit at the library or your local bookstore, flip through magazines or books, and find which styles and designs make your heart sing. What colors or patterns stand out to you? Which images bring a smile to your face? Look honestly through the pictures and find designs and styles that truly make you happy, not what you think will please others. This is about you and the space you will create memories in with your friends and family. And you can bring value to your life by bringing value to your environment.

As we start the home design process, I have planned paces for you to follow which will empower you to be your own master designer. The word pace means, "A single step taken when walking; consistent and continuous speed moving ahead" (Webster's Dictionary). Take each step as a pace, allowing each step to build on the next. Remember, pace not race. There are seven paces in all. Let's get started!

Pace One: Defining Your Style

With your mission statement in mind, grab your notebook and let's begin "Pace-One" by defining your style. A tip to discovering your style is to take a trip to your local furniture store. Often, furniture stores will create design styles and, by strolling through the store, you will gain clarity as to what styles best suit you. Walk around the store and find what you love. If a certain piece catches your eye, find out which style it is and use it to help define your style.

My dear friend Brenda loves western and, while she is an elegant woman, loves a little bling in her life. When designing her home, I defined her style as "Western Elegant" because, though Brenda loved the western feel, she didn't like anything rustic, country or old.

Allow yourself the freedom to combine styles such as modern/traditional, European/country, eclectic/contemporary-bling, old-world charm with a twist, farm house/chic or just plain clean and simple. It is not hard and even more, it can be fun! A peaceful, New York loft feel with a Texas twist works for my townhome. Knowing your personal style preferences will lay the foundation for each of the rooms in your home.

Once you have accomplished this first "Pace," begin eliminating the items in your room that don't align with your overall vision. This will allow you to maximize your time. Good design is all about the "edit" (managing what stays and what goes). If you are presently living with many "hand-me-downs," begin the edit by replacing each item with pieces true to the creativity placed inside of you.

Pause and Ponder

Now it is time to pause. Grab your notebook and begin to journal your reflections from these last few pages. What has jumped out to you the most as you have been reading? Write down the purpose and "design dream" you have for each room. Measure each room, being sure to include the height of the ceiling and the size of the windows in your measurements, and then write these measurements in your notebook with your room descriptions. This notebook will serve as a storage book for paint selections, receipts, fabric samples and more. Keep it with you when you are visiting different show rooms or furniture stores. Next, draw a depiction of your rooms using graph paper, keeping in mind the purpose for each space and mission for your home.

Pace Two: Where to Begin

"The beginning is the most important part of the work." -Plato

There is a basic rule when beginning any design project: know where you are starting and what the end purpose will be. The master suite and the foyer (entryway) are excellent places to start the design process for your home.

Regarding the foyer, what do you want your first impression to be? Do you want it to be cluttered and chaotic? Most likely not, yet if your entryway is crowded with coats, toys, or backpacks, you are unknowingly communicating to visitors your life is a little "out-of-control." However, candles and flowers resting on a small table are welcoming and communicate warmth and a sense of wellbeing. A colorful, patterned rug and soft lighting will set the tone for the rest of your home. No matter if you have a grand staircase or a small entry, setting the stage is important.

If you're starting with a clean, empty space, it may work best to start at the end. For example, if you have a pillow, art you love, or fabric you wish to add later, these elements will inspire the whole design. Seeing the end will help you with the beginning. So, if possible, clear your room completely before starting your space design.

The Master Suite

Every woman should fall asleep and awake looking at something beautiful, something that brings a smile to her lips. However, the master suite is often the room most neglected. Many times, I have explored a home only to discover the master bedroom has been seemingly forgotten in comparison to the children's rooms and other areas.

The master suite is not the place for laundry, photo projects, office work, or computer time. No, the master bedroom is to be a place of retreat, a burden-free zone, without work or photos of kids and parents.

Think about the purpose of your bedroom. Is it to find rest and relaxation? If so, only make room for items that invoke feelings of rest, leaving you with a sense of wholeness and relaxation. However, if the purpose of the master suite is to connect with your spouse and foster romance, then soft music, candles, and comfy bedding will be important. The important thing is to decide what you would like the outcome of your room experience to be and begin with this goal in mind. Design with purpose.

Start by putting your bed at the most visible wall. The bed should be the first thing you see when you enter the master suite, and since the bed is the largest piece in the room, work all other furniture pieces around it. Note: as a rule, work all pieces around the largest furniture piece for each room. Bedside tables and lamps should match if you want a balanced feel. But if balance is not your style, mix it up!

Stop for a moment: go to your bedroom (take a paper and pen with you) and write down the things you like about your room and the things you don't like. Is this room serving me? Is this room meeting my needs? What are you feeling? Is your room "over-done" or heavy? Is there laundry on the bed? Envision what you want to see, feel, and experience when you walk into your bedroom. Does this room align with your vision and lifestyle?

Prioritizing *You* in Design

I met Jana, one of my first clients, in a nail salon. Jana was the mother of three sweet little girls (triplets) who kept her busy. She invited me to her home because she really needed some help (*help* in her case was an understatement).

Upon my arrival, torn furnishing, stained carpets, and complete chaos greeted me. Jana's triplets were now four, and it was time to make some needed changes to her home, but she didn't know where to begin. I immediately recommended to Jana we begin in the master suite. I knew it would be important for them to have a place of retreat and rest while we worked on other areas of the home. Our inspiration for their bedroom was Jana's love for bed and breakfasts and the color blue.

Jana and her husband needed to leave town on business and, while they were away, I was free to complete the master suite renovations. Upon their return, Jana was anxious to see the result. I quickly received a phone call from Jana who, through tears of joy, told me it was the most beautiful room she had ever seen. "This room is more than I could have ever asked for," she said in a trembling voice.

After this experience, I began to see design was more than *stuff*—it was the heart. We went on to do her entire home. As we went room by room, she and her husband always had a place of retreat—the master suite.

Addressing one room at a time will ensure your design process is manageable. Again, design is about pace, not a race, which gives you a sense of reward and completion. No two homes are alike, and you may be blessed with a small and cozy home. If that is the case, you may need to design other spaces in your home to meet your "living" needs. For example, you might want a nook for reading in the bedroom, a small closet with a desk, or a table for crafts and sewing.

Prioritize how you will live in every space. Whether big or small, design your space to serve you best.

Pace Three: Painting with Purpose

By now, I am sure you are aware of how much freedom and support my parents gave me in the area of decorating. As a teen, I would practice my painting and design skills on anyone who would let me. My friends would allow me to paint ivy and butterflies on their walls, and I would rearrange the furniture and hang artwork for my mom's friends.

On one occasion, when I was 16, my parents were traveling, and I decided to update the family bathroom. I selected the colors for my project: tangerine orange and lemon yellow. But I needed to apply wallpaper over the pre-existing wallpaper, which was made with a fuzzy material. I had never installed wallpaper, but I thought, "How hard could this really be?"

I began to see design was more than *stuff*—it was the heart.

After purchasing some lovely paper featuring green ivy and yellow flowers (it was the 70s!), I began. The result was pleasing, however, the next morning all the wallpaper I had carefully hung was now completely peeled off and covered in fuzz! The fuzzy paper had caused my wallpaper not to adhere properly. What a mess! Mom and Dad arrived home to one more of Deb's design projects gone awry. Thankfully, my mom was humored by the situation and she hired a wallpaper installer to finish the job. And, to this day, I still love wallpaper. The additional texture and pattern can add so much to any space.

When designing your rooms, always consider what type of wall-coverings or paint colors will best enhance the overall look. Keep in mind, if your ceilings are low, it will be best if they are a light shade in a flat finish. Further, adding trim or crown molding to a room will significantly improve the space.

Paint is the greatest tool in your designer toolbox, yet it can also be the greatest frustration for clients. When it comes to selecting the right color, here are a few tips. First, it's important to look at your home as a whole. Choose a main trim color and neutral wall color to use throughout your home. Though you are only working on one room at a time, as it pertains to paint color, select the main color you wish to work with. One basic color and two accent colors work best for most homes.

Many people like the same colors their entire life, however, for some their favorite colors may change over time. Think about how long your color has been your favorite. Remember, the shade and hues are just as important as the actual color. You may have loved pink as a child and now, you can't live without red from the same color family!

Also consider the lighting in the room. Does the room have a lot of windows or is there little to no natural light? This will influence the colors you select. If your walls are going to be dark and dramatic, your bedding, furniture choices, and window coverings will need to be lighter in order to create contrast. Think of it as room drama. Choose to either have the walls or the décor be the dramatic element in the space.

When planning the accessories, think of it like planning your jewelry for an outfit, but you first have to pick the outfit! Another design idea is to create a room in all the same color using varying shades. The choices for painting and wall-coverings are numerous, but have fun with the process and don't forget the ceiling and flooring.

As you are considering the wall color and design, it may also be advantageous for you to learn how to read a Color Deck from your local paint store. If you select your color from the bottom of the paint card (the darkest shade on the strip), you will be able to move up the color strip to the shade you like. For example, if you want a brown, tan rather than one that is pink or golden, select the color at its darkest shade so you will be able to see the red or the gold in the darkest tone. If you locate true dark brown, as you move up the color strip, you will find the perfect tan.

Now, while utilizing these few tips may help you discover your favorite color, it is essential that you test and sample the colors in a small area of your wall before you commit to the whole process. Colors look different depending on the lighting and placement.

Visit your local paint shop or a model home and ask which color or colors are the most popular right now for interior walls. You will also need to select a paint finish, satin or flat. A satin finish works best if you have small children. But a flat finish shows less shadows and is great for touch-ups because it covers wall flaws best. If your walls are a "Wow" color, the result of this room will need to be loud and bold.

When choosing a color for your walls, realize it is much safer to begin with a softer tone, knowing you can later transition to something more dramatic. View colors like weights—they need to be balanced. If you decide to use a heavy or dramatic paint for the walls, balance it by selecting lighter finishes for your furniture. Or, if you have lighter wall colors, you can choose more dramatic or darker furnishings. Finally, pick the color that sings to you and remember it is only paint!

Pace Four: The Big and Small

I was five when my dad decided to fulfill my childhood dream of owning a pony. My dad found me the most adorable white Shetland pony that I named, Silver. We didn't own a truck however and, because of this, bringing Silver home was going to be interesting. My dad decided to take the back seat out of our 1954 Ford sedan and he stuck the pony right in there. During the drive home, Silver's behind busted out the back glass, but thankfully, he was uninjured. While my little pony did not quite fit into that little sedan, the experience was worth it for me. I sure did enjoy riding Silver all around our home, all the while wearing my little cowgirl outfit!

While this story is a funny example of the importance of scale, I often enter a home only to find the sofas, like Silver's backside in that little sedan, are completely out of scale with the entirety of the room. Many times, I find the sofa is too small or too big and, like

Goldilocks, the size needs to be just right.

When you place furniture in a room, you must have approximately three feet of walking space for flow, however, you can group furniture pieces together like two chairs with a small table. One tip is to use blue painters tape in order to map out the correct placement, all the while remembering that each room should look lived in, not staged.

After you have measured your space, you can compare the measurements with the pieces you are considering for purchase. Many furniture stores provide assistance in this area and, if you are making a large purchase, they will send someone to your home to assist you in how to create the best scale and furniture placement for your room.

But not only is it important to consider the scale and flow of your rooms, it is also important to continually remind yourself of what your use or purpose is for each room. How do you need the room to serve those who live there? How many people would you like to be able to seat at one time? Is there a flow for conversation in the room or is it better for watching television?

Again, when it comes to furnishings, neutral colors are the safest choice for sofas. Yet with chairs you can select bolder colors from prints to solid fabrics (solid colors are always in style), allowing the art and accent pillows to bring the room to life. In the average home, the living room is the largest room, and an excellent place to let your personality shine through books that reflect you, fun artwork and framed photos. For additional ideas, explore nice hotels and study the way they spice up a room or how they add the finishing touches to public areas. Remember, the room is a reflection of who lives there!

Pace Five: Window Treatments

"Adopt the pace of nature: her secret is patience."
-Ralph Waldo Emerson

If you are on Pace Five, you have already completed four paces and are well on your way to completing the transformation you desire. And while I am sure the vision and goal you have for your home is well worth the time and energy you are putting into the process, be sure to take time to not only reflect upon your journey but also savor your experience. Good design takes time and though design shows can make it look like you can do it all quickly, I usually work an average of one year or more with most clients.

It is now time to address your windows. Windows truly are the eyes of the room and window treatments can either cause rooms to look fabulous or disastrous. While shutters and shades may be convenient, they impede the flow of natural lighting. This is why I love "good old" draw drapes. There is nothing better than fully opening the window treatments in order to let the light shine through. Window treatments are the crowning glory for any room and come in a variety of colors and fabrics. Further, by properly placing your treatments, you can create the allusion that the window is grander than it really is. A tip is to hang the treatment on the wall approximately five to ten inches above the window and allow the treatment to hang outside the window frame with a width of ten inches to each side of the window. This will give the overall impression of a larger window.

The windows are also the perfect place to add drama! Window treatments come in many colors and textures, and ready-made window treatments have come a long way. Nowadays, you can choose anything from burlap for texture, to satin for shine. Silk and linen treatments work best if you enjoy a lighter look, but velvet (in any color) adds a bold and formal feel. I love adding lots of color and pattern through window treatments, and the kitchen is a great place to start. Allow yourself to be creative as you dress the eyes of your room.

In addition to window treatments, accent pillows add a punch of color and can bring your look together. Pillows and throws add design and texture, so be bold with your choices and let the colors shine. Remember, pillows do wear quickly and will need to be replaced often. Because of this, take a quick inventory of your pillows every now and then to determine if it is time to replace them.

Pace Six: The Art of Light

"God spoke: 'Light!' And light appeared. God saw that light was good." (Genesis 1:3, MSG)

Lighting is essential and is the "candle on the birthday cake" of any space. There is a vast assortment of lighting looks such as task lighting, overhead lighting, mood lighting, and dimmers, which allow you to adjust the light in order to create a specific mood. Truly, the design of light fixtures is more important today in the decor of your home than ever before. If you desire to update the look of your home, you can simply replace your light fixtures for a dramatic effect. Lighting is key to setting a design style.

I also love lamps and there is a vast and artful selection of styles to reflect any personal design. Now, lamps need not match unless you want a formal feel or if they are sharing a table space such as an entry table with two lamps to the right and left of a mirror. Lamps are like art, reflecting your personal taste. You can even mix periods, metals, glass, color, and style. Spice up a great shaped lamp by painting it. For example, painting an old lamp base white will help it to stand out, transforming the lamp's look. You can also check the shade and replace it if needed. Light should be layered.

Let the room glow with hanging light fixtures, but remember, scale is everything. Ask your local lighting store to help you with the best height and size for your light fixture. When visiting the lighting store bring your home journal with your design mission, and measurements (measure the height from ceilings to the floor and the room size). Lighting stores are a great resource for determining the best size for your fixture.

Lighting is further enhanced by the perfect placement of a mirror. Mirrors are a great way to reflect the woman of the house, while adding a splash of personality through the frame or design. A mirror should never float, so be sure to ground it by reflecting a beautiful vase or lamp. When it comes to artwork, the frames no longer need to match, however, if you are featuring a collection, it should include seven or more pieces of art and have a common thread: all blue and white, all floral art, or perhaps a collection of photos from family trips. Keep in mind your home should always be a reflection of you, not a generic trend.

To keep art in focus, be sure to choose pieces that are versatile and can be viewed from a distance or close proximity. If your art piece is busy or the subjects are small, hang the art in a place where it may be viewed more closely. In the same way, place larger art in an open area where it can be enjoyed from across a room. I love mixing and matching art and frames. Conversely, I try to avoid art that requires reading because the art piece and your eye should be telling the story. Ideally, a room will allow for one's eye to flow over the room without stopping to stare. And sometimes less is best.

Pace Seven: The Stuff and Placement of Life

Design is a process through which, by diligence and patience, your creative vision will come to life. Further, design is a means in which you will become more aware of how God has designed you as you are designing your personal space. You are giving value to yourself when you give time, attention, and value to your environment. By creating a welcoming home that reflects your values and your beauty, you will be creating an atmosphere that fosters love and welcomes new memories. The design and purpose of each room will become clearer as you work through each space in your home. Intentionally, filter out any items that do not add value or reflect your lifestyle.

Lighting is key to setting a design style.

"Let go of yesterday. Let today be a new beginning and be the best that you can, and you'll get to where God wants you to be."
-Joel Osteen

Two obstacles for quality design are collections and emotional attachment to stuff. One of my clients, Frances, lived in assisted living and, typically in assisted living situations the residents are not able to part with much of the collections and memorabilia they accumulate, thus their spaces are overcrowded and overwhelming to say the least. Frances was different. She was able to let go of the home of her past to embrace her present and design her new home to match her new lifestyle. Due to the lack of life clutter, her space was more inviting and became the hang out for all her new friends.

> You are giving value to yourself when you give time, attention, and value to your environment.

When working with a client, I have learned there is always the, "Oh no! That stays because it was my mom's!" Or, "We can't get rid of that 148-count spoon collection because it was my great Aunt Clara's." You get the point. Sometimes it is just time to let go!

Letting go is key to great design, although sometimes you may find a great piece of art and family history that is just waiting for display and will make a wonderful conversation piece. There have been many times I have dug up amazing treasures from my client's closets and storage areas. One time, I discovered a War Plane print that was signed by General Douglas MacArthur hiding under my client's bed! I hung the rediscovered art front and center in my client's family room and gave it the value and attention it deserved.

Now, we could not leave a topic of "stuff" without addressing the stuff most likely piled on your coffee table. Coffee tables sometimes end up being "stuff collectors," but with a little attention they can become wonderful flat canvases of art and function. I believe a coffee table should feature great books or a chess set, as well as room for coasters and beverages. Some clients enjoy featuring fresh flowers, candles, small art pieces or even a collection of lovely boxes. No matter the effect you are wanting to make, be sure to leave space to set items down like glasses, books or drinks. Remember, the best living space is the space that can be lived in!

Willie Nelson

Tragically, one year my mother-in-law experienced a house fire. We received a call that her home was ablaze, so we rushed over immediately. Our mom, in shock, sat in the neighbor's yard watching as the fire fighters strenuously worked to save what they could. Once we had received the "all clear" signal from the firefighters, we ventured into the remains of her once beautiful home.

The home had been burned in such a way you could still get into the bedroom, which only had smoke damage. The other half of the house was a total loss. We asked my mother-in-law what she wanted us to retrieve and her only reply was, "Please go and get me that picture of me with Willie Nelson!"

Mom had dated Willie before his long ponytail and she had a large photo of the two of them, her with a bee-hive and Mr. Nelson looking very young. The dear photo was framed and wrapped in plastic behind mom's dresser and this photo was the first thing she thought to save!

What items do you have that would be your first thought to save? While those items may not be what you want to showcase in your design, you can still value them as keepsakes, not wrap them in plastic and hide them away!

Getting rid of excess "stuff" is the best design tool of all. The space will be unsuccessful if you overload the eye through excess. The eye can only intake so much before it will "tune-out" the superfluous. Be sure only to retain items that not only bring beauty and design to your space, but also hold meaning and relevance in your life. Every room needs to have no more than three to five focal points because the eye also needs space to rest. Let your eye be your guide while you purposefully and diligently design each space.

Pause and Ponder

1. Define the style and purpose of your home.
2. Decide which room you will start with and list all the rooms based on highest to lowest priority. I recommend you complete one room at a time.
3. Plan a master color pallet even though you will be working on one room at a time. This will help the cohesiveness of your home.
4. Plan your furniture placement and ask for help when needed. Don't be afraid to add area rugs (art for your floors).
5. Maximize the overall look of your windows, the eyes of your room.
6. Decide how you will set the mood in your home through lighting and lamps.
7. Accessories are the jewelry of any space: art, books, pillows, and throws add that finishing touch. Now, go for it! Design and shine!

    The color Orange (Design) occurs between (Red) Home and yellow (Faith for Family), which is the next color we'll cover as it's essential to design your life canvas with all three colors in heart and mind.

YELLOW

Chapter Six

FAITH FOR FAMILY

"How wonderful yellow is. It stands for the sun."
-Van Gogh

Yellow is my favorite color and I tend to collect various articles in yellow. Two of my favorite paintings in my home feature yellow—a painting of Time Square with yellow taxis and a painting of a little girl standing on a beach wearing a yellow dress. My home has small yellow accents from yellow napkins to soft yellows and accent grays in my bedroom. Even my wedding colors were yellow, with yellow daisies.

Interestingly, recent studies have revealed how the color yellow affects us physically, stimulating mental processes and the nervous system, activating memory, and encouraging communication. Truly, yellow is a sensational color. Further, yellow is the brightest color of the rainbow, it's the color of gold and ripe lemons, and it stands for sunshine, smiles of optimism, and of course—happiness!

Colors are powerful and their impact on our everyday lives is vast. Thus, during our journey into family relationships, I want us to associate the color yellow with faith for the family. I believe family is the quintessential example of happiness and God's love. And our family relationships, though difficult at times, are so rewarding.

Family means having faith that you are forming love and trust on a day-to-day basis, as you share your life with those you love. One must always have faith as it relates to the family because the love you are cultivating today will carry you through to tomorrow. Faith for your family means, in the good times and the difficult times, you will always seek to believe the best about those you love, walking hand-in-hand with them through life. Hebrews 11:1 says, "Faith is the confidence that what we hope for will actually happen; it gives us assurance about things we cannot see" (NLT).

The family provides many opportunities to receive and

express love. However, sometimes when we are faced with hurts, disappointments, and setbacks, it is essential to apply the virtue of faith to our families—always believing in them and forgiving them. As we are on this journey together, let yellow become a symbol in your mind not only of happiness and optimism, but of faith for your family and children. Together, let's paint the world yellow through our faith.

"What can you do to promote world peace? Go home and love your family."
–Mother Teresa

When I was a young girl, we lived on a hog farm in Ohio. Though we mostly raised pigs, we had other animals too. One day, my dad took our pigs to auction and he returned with a baby goat. It was soft and creamy. Immediately, I fell in love with it and I named her Amy. She was so sweet. Kid goats attach quickly, and my Amy would cry loudly for me every night (she could be heard from the barn all the way up to the house and across the fields).

Now, my grandparents lived in a trailer next to our farmhouse and Amy's loud cries for me kept my grandpa awake. So, because my mother wouldn't let me sleep in the barn, the result was that no one slept. Yet, loud or not, she always stayed right by my side and was the best pet I have ever had.

I loved putting bows on Amy (I had an endless supply from the cemetery dump). She would wear old faded bows until she ate them off. However, shortly after her arrival, I discovered Amy was actually a boy goat and not a girl after all. This was very disappointing, but I still dressed her (I mean him) up like a girl. My brothers and I soon discovered if we tied her up with grass rope, the rope used for hay bales, we would have just enough time to hide before she chewed through the rope. Finally, free, she would come and find us and butt us with her head.

My dad came from a big family. He was the oldest of six children (I have 18 cousins on my dad's side alone). My grandfather came from a family of ten children and, though I have no idea how many cousins my dad has, I do know that everyone loved hanging out on our farm. We had a spirit of hospitality and my dad loved to cook.

One weekend, my Uncle Hoppy came up with the "bright" idea to barbeque Amy. So, they did. There was Amy, on our kitchen table, all covered in sauce. Of course, I could not eat Amy and it broke my heart that my dad let the others eat my goat. Later, my dad told me he was very sorry. I even received a lovely note from him on my wedding day telling me how proud he was of me and how very sorry he was for barbecuing my Amy. He asked me to please forgive him and I carried his note in my wallet for many years.

My father was not a bad man, he loved us and worked hard to give us a good life. But due to his own difficult upbringing, he was hard in some areas and unaware of the impact of his choices. Dad was raised in a coal mining camp in West Virginia and in those days, they raised kids the tough way—with a razor trap as their guide. My father's past home defined his future home, tough instead of tender. Whatever dad said was law. We never talked back and, if we did, a whipping was the answer.

Scars

Many times, adults carry scars from their past into their present and future. These are often from parents but, if we were honest, I believe we would realize our parents were doing the best they could. Most likely, they carried scars from their upbringing too. They simply tried to parent while still bearing their own burdens and childhood pain.

Personally, I have a scar from my past from when we were visiting my dad's Kentucky relatives in Greenup County. They were of Scotch-Irish decent, and one of them had just delivered a baby. The cloth diapers needed to be washed, so we were laundering them in the old, wringer washer on the front porch. I loved helping and watching the two ringers push the water out. Somehow, my small fingers went through the ringers, followed by my arm. I started screaming and pulling (I was fighting hard for the machine not to pull me in up to my elbow).

Finally, someone unplugged the washer and they were able to free my arm. I still have the scar, it's faint now, but there nonetheless. I didn't know better at the time. Today, I could look at the scar and be mad, blaming someone for letting a small girl use the wringer washer, but the only way for my scar to truly heal is through forgiveness.

Sometimes, we are unaware that we need to forgive and let go of hurts. But by putting our trust in God and receiving the great deposit of forgiveness God has freely given us, we too can be empowered to forgive. When we forgive, the things that scarred us as children, if we look closely, will have faded just like my old scar.

As a young girl, I was given many chores on the farm. My dad told me men liked to see calloused hands. I laugh at that statement now and I didn't raise my girls with that point of view. But today, by God's grace, I am able to find value in the way my parents raised me. It takes faith, but today, I value how God used my upbringing to make me a stronger and more resilient woman. I feel blessed to have the Mom and Dad I have. I honor my mother and father to this day and I love them dearly, but I will never eat goat!

God Knows

We are unable to select our family members and some parents may not deserve our honor, but we can still honor the position they have and value the relationship. By faith, we can see God is able to take a mess and make it a message. Even a hard childhood can produce value and faith in our lives if we turn our scars over to God and forgive.

The Bible says without faith it is impossible to please God, but have you ever thought of this verse in light of forgiveness? Forgiveness takes faith, a great amount of faith—faith that God knows your pain, faith that He is the God of justice, and faith that

He will heal your wounds and wipe away your tears. But receive this today: You can trust God.

Today, have faith and forgive—see your family through the lens of yellow. As you forgive and live with understanding, the yellow hue of your faith will brighten your life and the lives of those around you.

Yellow is Faith for Aging Parents

"Take care of any widow who has no one else to care for her . . . This is something that pleases God" I Timothy 5:3–4 (NLT)

In my family, aging gracefully is in the genes. I remember my great, great grandmother, Grannie Regions, living to be ninety-four. She would tell us stories about when the Native Americans would come to trade with her father and she would hide under her mom's dress, while her mom sat in her rocking chair.

Grannie had five names (Matilda, Urenie, Kelly Ann, Tidonia, Finley Regions) and eight daughters. Grannie lived with her daughter Elvira, in Louisiana, and my mom was faithful to visit her family there and express her love for them. Louisiana nights, however, were cold, and because it was always too dark to find the outhouse, Elvira's home had "slop-buckets." Slop-buckets were used like a midnight porta-potty, yet I could never bring myself to use one, just like I could never venture out into the woods—no matter how much nature was calling. The slop-buckets gave Grannie Region's home a peculiar smell, which was further enhanced by the fact she chewed sweet gum and dipped snuff.

I was nine years old on my family's last visit with Grannie. She was blind by this time and I thought, "If she is blind, she won't know I'm here." As always, my mom wanted me to give her a hug, but I didn't want to. Frankly, I was a little frightened by her and, even though she was asking for me, I avoided hugging her. Later, she fell and broke her hip—I never saw her again. I felt that if I had just given her a kiss and a hug, she wouldn't have passed away. Through this experience, I learned to always end a visit or a phone call with "I love you" or a hug because you never know if it will be your last.

At the time of this writing, my grandmother, "Mamaw," is still going strong at over ninety-five. With this genetic miracle of long life, I know that eventually I will be caring for my mother. But I also know that the dynamics between an aging parent and the child caring for them can feel like a tight rope at times—where boundaries are essential, and love must cover everything.

My husband was not ready for his mother to give up living on her own, but after she had a house fire that left her homeless as well as a stroke, it was time for her to move in with family. I watched as my sweet sister-in-law faced the dynamics of taking in my husband's mom. I realize every family needs to care for their parents in the way they feel is best. But again, according to 1 Timothy 5:3, it is the responsibility of the children to care for their aging parents. And with the shift in responsibilities, it is important to communicate expectations clearly and set boundaries. However, at the end of the day, the final decision regarding the parent's care should be upon the individuals who are giving the most care and taking on the greatest burden of responsibility.

"To care for those who once cared for us is one of the highest honors."
—Tia Walker

It is vital we connect with and value our aging parents. This will bring the beauty of yellow into those relationships. It's also important to remember that part of having healthy boundaries is learning how to "disconnect" when the demand of care is high. If you are the primary caregiver of aging parents, it is important to gather a support team that will encourage you, give perspective, and provide aid when it's needed.

In addition to having a support system in place, it's also essential to establish boundaries. I can recall a time when I volunteered to sit with my friend's aging mother. It was just going to be for a few hours, and I planned to read to her and encourage her. I thought it would be a breeze.

Before I went, my friend shared how after bringing her mother into their home, they discovered her mother was rather difficult. I didn't quite understand what she could mean by this, but she went on to explain how they had tried having her in their home saying, "It's not working out, she is hard to handle!" I soon discovered what the definition of "difficult" included. I was just barely in the room when I leaned in to adjust a blanket and I was almost bitten! Truly, this visit was more bite than breeze!

I share this because each family is unique with various challenges and, while you may not be fending yourself off from being bitten, wisdom is needed to know how to care for your aging loved ones. Pray you will know how to bring honor to your parents and to yourself when times are trying. As you view your family and your present circumstances, look for ways to add yellow to each new day.

Pause and Ponder

Now it is time to "Pause and ponder," so grab your journal and favorite cup of tea or coffee. If you have aging parents or grandparents, hold onto the good memories you have of them. When I was young, my Mamaw (grandmother) and I had a favorite hang-out place, Woolworth store in Lancaster, Ohio. We always enjoyed strolling through the store, followed by a lunch of BLT's and sodas.

Every year, my Mamaw would come to help my mom get ready for our first day of school. She always enjoyed buying me a brand-new dress and Woolworth was our place. One time as we were walking around, we noticed a large bin of panties in the center of the store. My Mamaw began to dig around the bin looking for her size. It must have been a good sale because she was very excited.

When my mother asked where we were, Mamaw replied, "Here we are! Just playing in the panties!"

Now, my Mamaw loved to laugh and she was so tickled over her comment, "We are playing in the panties," that she started her "jelly belly laugh." She laughed so hard that she cried and peed! But Mamaw didn't just make a little puddle of pee—no, it was a major puddle, right there in the middle of the store. I couldn't help myself and I began to laugh until tears ran down my cheeks. My mother was horrified to say the least!

Today, I hold this memory close to my heart now that my dear Mamaw has aged and time has stolen her laughter. But what about you and your family? Make a list of the funniest and fondest memories you have shared with your loved ones. Pause and ponder on these memories so that, when the gray season of life comes, you will be able to recall the more colorful times you have shared.

Honey, I'm Home!

No book about balancing our lives and defining our homes would be complete without touching on the husband and wife relationship. Now, I am the last person to say I have the answers regarding marriage, but I do believe giving your marriage value and choosing to stay connected to one another is key to creating a whole and a healthy marital relationship. And the connection we have or don't have with our home will directly impact our marriages, whether we realize it or not.

As a professional designer, my days are spent with clients shopping, working with contractors, and creatively crafting rooms. I have a home-office and when I am home, I often feel like I am still at work, and at my work I am the boss—so I boss. The challenge for me is finding a way to connect with my home so I can disconnect from my work. I don't believe in multi-tasking, and I feel it's important to learn how to disconnect from work-life in order to deliberately connect to home and family.

I know a wife greeting her husband at the door with his pipe and slippers are days gone by. However, the work environment your husband goes into each day could be highly competitive, maybe with an unkind boss, or labor intensive. How is the "Honey-I'm-Home!" for you? Is he hopping over toys, walking into stress and mess? Maybe he avoids coming home and goes to the gym or hangs out with the guys.

Make the Connection

In the movie, "Fried Green Tomatoes," Evelyn Couch, a woman trying desperately to improve her marriage, imagines greeting her husband at the door wearing plastic wrap when all Ed wanted was her fried chicken and a baseball game. I'm not saying you should greet your husband adorned in plastic, but a check in the mirror before his arrival never hurts. You may have a job that doesn't translate well to your home. Maybe it's hard for you to disconnect from work while you're at home or, maybe you're with children throughout the day so your husband often comes home to a "day-care" tone. Make it a priority to intentionally create a "relational-tone" with your spouse.

Connecting with my husband was always important to me so one day I decided to make a list of all the things I did around the home for my husband (this will look different for every marriage). I asked Terry to tell me which item on my list was the most meaningful to him. He shared with me that he felt loved when I cooked a meal, prepared his plate and served it to him. This act of service communicated value and love in his language. The nice part for me was that after a long hard day, I could manage this simple task easily. It empowered me to know, through this simple expression of service, I could connect with my husband, while not wasting time doing a lot of other tasks that were unnecessary and didn't "make the connection" for him.

Another area of connection for Terry is when I simply bring him a plate of snacks when he is watching a football game. It seems so easy to me, yet it makes him so happy!

Often, as women, we try to love and care for our men in the way we would want them to love and care for us. But according to proverbs, a woman builds her house wisely. Proverbs 24:3 says, "By wisdom a house is built, and by understanding it is established" (NLT). The principle here is that a woman of wisdom approaches her family and her home strategically. In the same way we are careful to study a recipe or create the right look for our home, we can approach our marriage with the heart of someone who is ready to learn and discover. As we do, we will brighten our homes with the happy yellow that comes through healthy connection.

Now, I have to admit, I'm a bit spoiled by my husband. He has always been quick to clean the dishes, make our bed, and do his own laundry. He definitely has a servant's heart. Did I always value that? No, I thought I needed to do all the cleaning and laundry. I thought, "Isn't that a wife's job?" And when it came to Terry's "presumed" roles, I had a long list: lover, accountant, spiritual leader, diligent worker, loving father and of course—romantic.

Does your husband have the all-too-elusive "romance-gene"? If he does, value it! I remember Terry buying me flowers, while I thought, "This is a waste of money! I would prefer a gift that doesn't die!" Do you think I received flowers again? Oh no, I didn't receive flowers for a long time!

Another time, I was sick, and Terry lovingly made me soup. I remember criticizing the soup—big mistake. Love cannot grow where there is criticism and a lack of value and respect. Love dies in a critical and judgmental environment. Rather than adding yellow to our relationships, criticism and judgment are like painting our canvas with black splotches.

Simone Signet once said, "Chains do not hold a marriage together. It is threads, hundreds of tiny threads which sew people together through the years." This statement gives value to the idea that the little investments and connections we make in our marriages are vital. For example, random acts of kindness, little pet names and pet words, not only add a colorful spice to any relationship, but they are the tiny threads that sew two hearts together in marriage.

We add yellow to our marriages, one small, yellow thread at a time. So, study your spouse. Approach them as if you just met them. Be ready and expectant to learn something new about who they are. Embrace the idiom "Never stop learning," as it relates to your marriage every day.

Men have a stronger need to disconnect from their work than women. When my husband comes home, it's unwise for me to bombard him with my questions and needs before he has had time to connect with our home. This was a hard lesson for me to learn. Now we have a chair in our home that is Terry's chair. And my husband needs his "Chair-time" after a long and hard day of work. But once Terry unwinds during "Chair-time," I know he can handle whatever I throw his way.

Creating a connection with your husband is invaluable and will bear fruit that lasts a lifetime. Learn how to disconnect from work, television, and cell-phones so that you can maintain an intimate connection with your spouse. Also, learn how to clearly and calmly communicate with your spouse in such a way that will unlock the secrets of his heart. What is "connection" for him? Ask him what makes him feel connected to you and you might be surprised. I know I was.

The color of your marriage may not look like anything you have ever seen and that is okay. Never expect your marriage to look like another marriage. Allow it to be the beautiful, unique color that God has designed it to be and watch love grow on your canvas of life!

Seeing Him in Yellow

As I mentioned earlier, the first time Terry expressed an outward interest in me, he decided to do it by wearing a yellow suit to church. He definitely caught my attention and I was smitten. However, I think the visual he made was such a lovely illustration of how we should view our husbands—dressed in yellow—symbols of hope, happiness, and faith for the future.

In marriage, we are afforded the opportunity to experience our husbands during their best and worst times, and, instead of trying to hide or ignore our husband's faults, we should cover our husbands in prayer and love.

1 Peter 4:7-8 says, "Be earnest and disciplined in your prayers. Most important of all, continue to show deep love for each other, for love covers a multitude of sins" (NLT). When we notice a fault or flaw in ourselves or our spouse, we may be tempted initially to become critical or bitter, but what if instead we covered them in prayer?

When we are strategic concerning how we approach and respond to the blemishes in our marriage, we'll find God is able to bring life and redemption to even the most difficult of situations. Why? Because "with God all things are possible" (Matthew 19:26b, NLT). Just like my Terry was dressed in yellow, your husband can be dressed in yellow too as you choose to honor him.

Yellow is Faith for Spouses

I have a pottery bowl that is a beautiful shade of ivory. It has two distinct stripes around it in a brilliant blue color. Its most distinguishing feature however is the large crack running down the side.

I purchased this bowl several years ago in Marshall, Texas, while I was traveling with my parents. We decided to stop at a pottery shop with several large crock stoneware mixing bowls. The bowls were much more than I could afford at the time, but I wanted one. I noticed in the clearance area there was the same bowl, but for a fourth of the price because the bowl contained a large crack on the outside finish. I decided to purchase the bowl because I knew I could easily turn the bowl around, so the crack would not show.

Today, I love the crack and I purposely turn the bowl around in order to see its blemish daily. Why, you might be wondering? Because it is a daily reminder to appreciate my marriage in its entirety—the good, the bad, the beautiful, and the messy. I hate to compare my sweet husband to a cracked bowl, but there are no perfect people and there are no perfect marriages. I used to focus on his flaws, but now I focus on him. I have learned to value and embrace my husband in every aspect, including his cracks!

Pause and Ponder

What are some of the ways you connect with your spouse? Take some time to prayerfully ask God how you can connect with your home each day.

How can you purposefully help your spouse connect with your home? Start discovering the answer to this question today by asking your spouse what two things you can do each day to make them feel loved. Like the sun, including yellow in your marriage will help it grow!

YELLOW

Chapter Seven

CHILDREN ARE SUNSHINE

Pablo Picasso once said, "Some painters transform the sun into a yellow spot, others transform a yellow spot into the sun." Yellow is a powerful color and how we choose to apply it to our daily lives is everything. If the color yellow stands for sunshine, smiles of optimism, and happiness, we should enthusiastically incorporate yellow into each day. But not only does yellow give us the sunshine, it also reminds us to have faith—specifically faith for family and for our children. Whenever you see the color yellow, remember to have faith for those you love and to be optimistic for the future. Faith is eternal, like family.

Looking at my childhood, I can see how important yellow must have been for my mom and dad. My parents truly wondered if I would ever mature past my childish and free-spirited ways. My mother and grandmother had big dreams for their little Debbie, but my school years did not look promising.

My first-grade teacher was the principal's wife and she had no problem sending me to the principal's office whenever I was upsetting her, which I hate to say was a lot. I don't remember being a bad child, I just possessed a creative mind that unfortunately got me into trouble. For example, there was a large tree in the front of our school and there were always squirrels playing in its branches. I could see this tree from the window in our classroom.

Often, I became lost in my daydreams as I was naming each squirrel and making up stories about their lives, while also imagining their "squirrel conversations." I would be so deep into my squirrel dialogues that I was completely unaware of what the teacher was saying or doing. On one such occasion, my teacher suddenly brought me back to reality by grabbing my arm so severely that her fingernails cut me.

Needless to say, I passed first grade. Third grade, however, was a different story. I walked to school each day, so my teacher would often have me stay after class to finish my work. She always had her eyes on me and even placed my desk next to her own. A delightful little boy named Jamie also sat next to me and we had so much fun flipping pencils and throwing paper wads. My poor teacher!

One day, I did not want to stay after school, so I told my teacher that my grandma had a heart-attack and our family was going to see her. She let me go home, but the next time my mom came to the school the teacher asked, "How is your mother doing since her heart attack?" Oops! It was becoming clear that little Debbie didn't like the third-grade teacher or the third grade. Art was the one thing I did enjoy because it was a creative outlet for me.

There was one time when my teacher's daughter arrived with flowers for her mother's birthday and I heard our teacher saying, "Why did you bring this vase? It's too special to have in my classroom!" The vase truly was lovely and so was the mixed bouquet. Decorated with floral designs, the vase had a milky soft pink finish. I can still see it today. After much persuasion from her daughter, our teacher relented and allowed the flowers to stay in the classroom.

Now, we had a classroom rule: you must put your coat on in the coatroom. I'm sad to this day that I did not follow this rule. I grabbed my coat and, after swirling it around, the vase came crashing to the floor. My teacher wept. Later, she told my parents that there was no way I was going to be passing the third grade. Further, she told my parents that she felt like I needed to be seen by a doctor (and not a medical one). The blessing came, however, when our family decided to move to Ohio, two months before the school year ended.

Once we arrived in Ohio, I was placed in an "old-time" school, with old fashion values and little did I know the joy and love that awaited me in the fourth grade through the kindness of Miss Sweeny. My parents were informed that she was gifted with children like me, and she was. She was the kindest person I had ever met, and I loved her. She had three chins and snow-white hair, but she loved me, and she loved teaching. She spent countless hours teaching me how to read, and I began to love school.

I still had a vast imagination that steered me towards trouble, however. For example, one day our school bus broke down, making us late to return home. I knew my mother would be sick with worry and I thought it would be too boring to simply tell her that the old school bus had broken down and we had to wait while they made the repairs. No—surely, she needed a riveting tale.

On our farm, we had a long lane that connected the road to our house, so after the bus dropped me off I had some time to think of a better story. I decided to tell her that a drunk driver hit our bus. I thought, "Yes, that sounds much more exciting." Further, I thought I should have an injury to go along with my story. So, I hit myself in the head with a rock (my poor mom). Well, just like all the times before, my story found me out. Our family decided to go out for burgers that evening and who do you think was there— the bus driver! As I was sliding down in my seat, I heard my dad asking the bus driver about the accident. Later, I had to write 100 times, "I will not lie."

Faith for Children

These stories seem so comical to me now, but at the time, I know my parents were truly concerned for me and they had no idea how I was going to turn out. In sharing these stories with you, it is my desire that you would be encouraged to have faith for your own children and for the stories you may currently be experiencing that right now might not feel so comical.

Psalm 127:3 says, "Children are a gift from the Lord; they are a reward from Him," (NLT). But it takes faith on the part of the parent to believe this truth during difficult seasons. I'm sure that my parents are still shocked that I became successful in business and in life. You may need a lot of faith right now for your children, but I want to encourage you to pray and to believe that God is in control of their future.

James 5:16b–18 says, "The prayer of a righteous person has great power as it is working. Elijah was a man with a nature like ours, and he prayed fervently that it might not rain, and for three years and six months it did not rain on the earth. Then he prayed again, and heaven gave rain, and the earth bore its fruit" (ESV). In this verse, James is sharing with believers that our prayers are powerful. The King James Version says, "The effectual fervent prayers of a righteous man avail much." According to the Webster's Dictionary, the word fervent means: exhibiting or marked by great intensity of feeling: zealous. Some synonyms of fervent are blazing, passionate, impassioned, vehement, ardent, and intense.

The point is that prayers for our children need to be focused, fervent and full of faith. James 5:16 does not say that the effectual "worries" of a righteous mom avail much, but the effectual "prayers" of a righteous mom avail much. Let your prayers be like Picasso's strokes of yellow sunshine on the lives of your children, because not only are a mother's prayers powerful, her faith is powerful too.

When praying for your children, it is important to find scriptures from God's word that you can stand on and pray over your children. Isaiah 54:13 says, "All your children shall be taught by the Lord, and great shall be the peace of your children" (NKJV). When the apostle Paul writes, "Being confident of this, that He who began a good work in you will carry it on to completion until the day of Christ Jesus," (Philippians 1:6, NKJV) we can be confident that the good work God began in our children will be completed. Never lose hope—believe and pray.

Here is a tip to ponder, plant seeds of wisdom in the hearts of your children by teaching them the proverbs. Pick verses that will relate to your family. Study the meaning with your children and help them apply wisdom to their lives.

A Pop of Connection

My parents raised my siblings and me with substantial freedom. Our farm was large, and my mother would pack us a lunch, so we would be able to run around the farm all day, only returning at dinnertime. In fact, my brother once fell asleep in my corn crib for two hours. (His nap happened while the silos were being filled.) My mom couldn't find him, and she was convinced he had been buried alive in the grain. As the men were about to begin emptying the silos, my brother woke up. The silos were spared and so was our freedom!

One day, my mother needed to take my brothers into town, so she allowed me to have a friend over to keep me company. The kitchen was all mine and on this special day I decided to make popcorn-balls. We read the recipe and began popping corn. The recipe called for 12 cups of "popped" popcorn, but somehow, we missed this important detail and measured out 12 cups of "un-popped" popcorn. We were so happy and giggly that we didn't notice our mistake until we added the syrup. There simply was not enough to make all the balls, so we made more! We worked and worked, until we were tired of making popcorn balls; we were running out of places to put them!

Never lose hope—believe and pray.

Suddenly, I realized my mom was going to be home soon and not only were there popcorn balls everywhere, but there was a weird sound whenever we walked across the floor on our increasingly sticky feet. Getting one of my "creative" ideas, I decided, in order to clean the kitchen floor, we needed to squirt dish soap all over it. Using dish towels, we began to skate across the kitchen floor! My mother's arrival was imminent, and I didn't want her seeing the soap suds floating in the air, so I decided to lock her out of the house.

We never locked the door at home so, as you can imagine, my mom was not pleased to return to a locked house. She called out, "Deborah Bernice! What are you doing?" I finally let my mom into the house and thankfully she thought the entire situation was funny. She had perspective and was able to respond to me rather than react. Because of her wisdom, she and I are able to fondly recall this memory. This relational connection brought more yellow into our home, and more popcorn balls than we could eat!

Remember, children are little adults and they take a lot of connection time and energy. Even if you have a meaningful connection with your children a majority of the time, because of the demands of life, you may still feel like you are unsuccessful in your parenting. I think raising small children is like trying to stay on the top of a rolling log floating over rapids. Just don't fall off!

Yellow for JELL-O

In addition to connecting with our children, it is essential that we learn how to respond to each situation, rather than react. One morning, I was awakened by the presence of my six-year-old granddaughter, Devon, who had climbed onto my bed. As my eyes opened and I was slowly coming to consciousness, I became aware that my hand was being placed into a bowl of bright, red JELL-O. "Is the JELL-O done, Grammie?" Devon asked eagerly, as she squished my fingers deeper into the bowl. So, there I was. Do I react or respond? With a bowl full of bright red JELL-O, Devon sat excitedly perched on my cream-colored Martha Stewart quilt. I calmly responded, "Yes, sweetie, the JELL-O is done," and I carefully took the bowl from her.

Now, I have an advantage over parents that are in the midst of raising their children. That advantage is called perspective. As a grandmother, I know that the antics of a six-year old pass in a flash, and I know that this "JELL-O moment" is no big deal. The value that I place on my granddaughter is more important than my Martha Stewart quilt. But if I play this scenario in my mind when I was a Mom to three little girls, I know the outcome would have been more reactive due to lack of perspective.

A reaction is like an explosion; it blows up and leaves wreckage behind. If I could, I would turn young moms into grandmas for a day in order to show them how fast children grow and how sweet the moments really are. Having the proper perspective will allow you to bring the color of yellow into a home with children.

Also, as a grandmother, I am aware that children are more

capable than you realize. When you view your child from a close proximity each day, it is easy to lose perspective on what they are truly able to do (just like it is hard to perceive when they have grown an inch). I remember giving Marley, one of my sweet granddaughters, a glass to drink from. Her mother quickly reacted saying, "She can't drink out of that!" However, little Marley held the glass and was able to drink from it just fine.

Try to take a step back from your child and view them more objectively. Ask God to renew your perspective and responses towards your children, letting Him help you infuse your family with faith and yellow.

Snake in the House

While it is important to always choose our responses, there are times when things happen so fast you can't think it through and need to react. When I was three years old, we lived in Jones Creek, Texas, and one of my favorite activities was to jump over a large hole that was in the backyard. The hole had a poorly fitted lid and I loved jumping over it repeatedly. My mother was very pregnant during this time with my twin brothers, and she would often watch from the back porch as I played.

But, one day, as I went to jump, the lid flipped off and I went screaming down the hole. My mother, with a lightning-fast reaction, cleared four steps off the back porch in order to save me. She was able to get me out unharmed, but the physical exertion of her heroic act caused the twins' birth shortly thereafter.

I can remember another time in that same house when a "reaction" was needed. After returning home one day, we discovered a snakeskin hanging on our front porch. We didn't think much about it, until later that day when my mom reached into her drawer and instead of a hairbrush, she discovered a coiled-up rattlesnake. She quickly retrieved her three babies and left the house while the neighbor, who had heard her screams, came running with a gun in-hand. Shortly after we heard a "pop" and our neighbor emerged holding a dead snake.

These stories are a sobering reminder that there are times when a reaction might be required of us. Remember when Jesus stormed the temple with a whip in-hand? He readily rid the temple of the dishonest men and declared, "My Father's house will be a house of prayer." Did Jesus wonder what his disciples might think, or did He worry that He would lose some of His followers, or how this would affect His ministry? No! Instead, He reacted with bold determination. What would have happened if Jesus had not reacted in this situation? What would have happened if my mom had not reacted when I fell or when she saw the snake?

In the same way, we should not worry about how our family members will feel or what a friend might say. Trust God to lead you to know when it is time to respond and when it is the time to react. Think of a large forest fire that causes great destruction and yet it could have been put out when it was just a spark if someone had known to take action. Song of Solomon 2:15 says that it is the little foxes that spoil the vine. Even the smallest snake in your home needs a reaction. Guard the yellow of faith in your home by keeping the foxes and snakes out!

Yellow Nannies

According to the United States Department of Labor, the job market for Nannies is expected to increase by 14% in the next several years. There seems to be a high demand for nannies! I believe that one of the reasons nannies are so successful is because they see childcare as a job and not something that is inconsequential. And just like you can learn house cleaning tips from a hotel-maid, you can learn child rearing tips from a professional Nanny.

Growing up, we would occasionally have a nanny stay with us when my parents traveled. I always enjoyed it when the nanny was present because she was structured and approached daily chores and routines systematically. Our nanny would always have food on the table when we arrived home from school, so we would start our homework after we ate. Nannies know that children love structure and routine. Children appreciate knowing what they can expect and what will be expected of them. On the other hand, children feel insecure if the plan changes every day or even worse—there is no plan! Can you imagine being in a job where you had no idea what the boss was going to have you do each day or what he or she expected of you? In contrast, if you arrive for a day of work knowing what the plan will be, your chances of success significantly increase.

Like a nanny, young moms will benefit from creating a plan or a list of desired goals for each day. Start by identifying the areas of stress in your life or in your parenting. Ask yourself, on a scale from one to ten, how busy are you and how busy is your child? Stress and an overly busy life can zap the brightness of yellow out of your home.

As a young mom with three girls, three car pools, a growing business, a husband, a home to keep, and meals to make, I sometimes found myself in survivor-mode. It sounded like this: "You need what for school tomorrow! What class? Take you to what school play to see who? What party and where do they live? Honey, no I can't help paint your mom's kitchen! My parents are coming to stay for a week!" Just writing this list makes my stomach feel like it is in knots! In seasons like this, I felt like there was no yellow in my life.

If you feel the way I did, prayerfully ask God how you can de-stress your life and parenting. Guard your home against "Too-Busy and Hurry-Rush." This spirit tries to creep into our homes and creates a tone that says, "We are only valuable when we are busy or being productive." Ask yourself, "What activities need to go in order for our home to be less stressful?"

God did not design our lives to be busy and stressful. The goal is that as a mom you will be able to break free from "survival-mode" and enter into "savor-mode" where you truly enjoy your family and your children. Cherish the precious children that have been entrusted to you by taking time to ponder your path. You can begin adding more yellow if you purpose to create a plan to decrease stress in the identified areas. If you don't know where to start, find another mom or a mentor that you trust and ask them to help you get started. Once you have "de-busied" your life, you can plan time for stories, making cookies, and connection, approaching your parenting strategically.

Know Your Limits

It is vital to claim your ground as a parent; however, this cannot happen until you set boundaries for your children or grandchildren. Children need to understand limits. This happens when you teach them to respect your personal space, whether it's mom's purse, mom and dad's bedroom or a closet. Setting boundaries for your children will foster an attitude of respect and honor in their lives.

Decide on your house rules and keep them simple but be very specific. Some ideas might be: "no technology" zones, a specific clean room time, using kind words, and treating others the way you want to be treated. Keep the rules positive. You may even want to call a family meeting to create limits that will specifically address your family's needs and explain to your children why you are setting each house rule. Remember, this process will look different for everyone.

As a mom with young children, I had boundary issues with my girls in restaurants. So, in order to practice boundaries, for a period of time, I planned trips to McDonalds. My girls loved McDonalds, and it was an easy place to leave if my girls began to misbehave. For example, if my girls didn't listen and misbehaved, I would calmly tell them that we were leaving. I only had to do this twice. My girls quickly learned the expected behavior when dining out.

When creating house rules be sure that the consequences are always clearly defined. Also, if you have a difficult teen in your home, you may want to get a mediator—someone who will clearly define and communicate the house rules from an objective vantage-point. During one season, our family needed to use a mediator (a mediator can even be a friend of the family), who helped us set clear boundaries with our teen. Most importantly, when it comes to boundaries, be sure that at the end of the day, your child knows you love them.

Boundaries for Technology

Setting boundaries have never been harder than it is now. Today, families are inundated with technological distractions, and most families find it challenging to build valuable relationships with family members when there are no limits on technology. This is why it's important to foster genuine opportunities for connection and for relating by creating "tech-free" zones with your family. Undivided time is precious for children of all ages.

One day, my lovely daughters and I were having lunch when an important client called me. I answered the call, which only lasted a few seconds, and when I looked up I noticed that all my daughters were now texting—heads down, looking at their phone. This moment struck me as such an oddity. Here we were, spending time together at a charming restaurant, and yet we were being sucked into a world of hi-tech diversions, where relationships lose their color. It was as if our family was being digitally re-imaged to remove some of the yellow.

On another occasion, I was enjoying lunch while also people watching. The restaurant was very nice, with white table clothes donning the tables and wonderful service. As I was admiring my surroundings, I noticed a mom leading her two sons towards their table. It was such a curious sight to see her pushing their shoulders forward while the young boys never looked up from their iPads. I can only imagine that this mother's original intent was to spend quality time with her sons, while also enjoying an exquisite lunch. But sadly, this did not happen because the boys never put down their iPads and boundaries were not present. It is important that we don't let a false sense of connection replace true and genuine connection.

Yellow Teens

God loves your children more than you do. So much that He gave His Son, Jesus Christ, for the redemption of your son or daughter. There was a day that I had to lay my teen at God's feet and rely solely on His love for her. I was tired and my Terah was determined to live life her way.

I had three children, thus God blessed me with three stages of rebellion: I have had the stubborn and willful toddler, the teenager that was so out of control that we would change the code on our house alarm each night, and the adult child who temporarily decided to be an atheist.

Rebellion in a child or a grown child is always difficult, however, I think dealing with it in a teen is the most challenging. One lovely October day, I was alone and on a walk. I was praying for Terah at the time. As I was praying, I felt close to God as I was surrounded by nature, and while lovely yellow leaves were blowing around me a deer walked by. In this moment, I felt connected with my heavenly Father. Sadly, my sweet daughter was in rebellion, and I desperately needed to give the burden of our circumstances to the Lord.

As I was walking, I noticed a large oval rock (approximately five feet long) in the middle of the field. I picked up a smaller rock and began to carve out the words, "Hope for Terah" and I left it there—I left the burden of her soul at God's feet. I left a part of me there as well, the part that had manipulated, preached, nagged, arranged and conspired. If you are a mom, you may know what I am talking about.

For example, I would take her to dinner only after she had attended church, or I would buy her books that I thought would "fix" her problem. But the day I carved "Hope for Terah," I decided to let go of her soul and, as I did, my "Mommy Savior" mentality left my heart. In the days that followed, when I was tempted to worry, I would see the picture of this event in my mind and I would remember that God was truly in charge of her life. I would let go again and let God. By doing this, I was putting a boundary on myself and choosing to have faith for my children.

Pause and Ponder

Now it is time to "Ponder" so grab your journal and that favorite cup of tea or coffee. Staying connected with our children is not always easy, but with a little strategy, you can make it work.

When I was building my business, my youngest daughter, Tessa, was a busy teenager who was active in basketball. In order to spend time with her, I decided that I would get up at five every morning, so we could have breakfast together before she left for practice (thinking back, I am amazed she wanted to get up early too). One day, she shared with school friends that she had a 5:00 a.m. breakfast date with her mom every morning. They could not believe she would do this just to have mom-time.

Another way we connected was by playing chess, and we had a creative way to play an ongoing chess game. I had a little glass frog that I would place on the board when it was her move. I would make a move throughout the day and she would see the frog and make her move. The games often went on for days, although sometimes we sat down in the evening and finished it together.

All this to say, how you bring the brightness of yellow into each relationship will require a different approach for each individual. Take a closer look at who you want to connect with and create a plan. Ask, how do I connect best with this person? What do we enjoy doing together? What do I need to disconnect from so I can connect with them? Make your plan fun and make your connections often. They don't need to be major events—remember, it is the little threads in life that bind!

When a painter's masterpiece is created, it doesn't happen with one big stroke of the brush. Use lots of little, intentional, meaningful strokes to brighten your relationships with more yellow, inviting the Master artist into the process. Ephesians 2:10 says, "For we are God's Masterpiece. He has Created Us anew in Christ Jesus, so we can do good things he has planned for us long ago" (NLT).

A Single Yellow Rose

In today's society, the marrying age is much older than it once was. I was married at 19, but that was even four years older than my mother who was married at 15. Whether you are single or a widow living alone, you can make your home and relationships all they can be through faith and connection.

With all of the technology that's available today, such as Skype, Face-time, and texting, it may seem like you are developing meaningful relationships, but there is no substitute for real face-to-face connection. Being able to have meals together, to see and touch the people that you love is invaluable. So, with that said, what is a single way you can add yellow to your life? Take inventory of the friendships that you already have and invite them to start a dinner club with you. Perhaps your church may offer small groups, so join a group, and start building meaningful relationships.

How important is design for the single lady? I believe it is more than important—it is essential. I have a friend named Jenny, who oversees missionaries. She shared with me that once she had a young single woman named Sally, who was doing wonderful work serving in Japan. Unfortunately, Sally desired to quit the mission field. This missionary was successful, and many people were being led to Christ through her efforts, yet she felt discouraged.

Jenny knew Sally had a heart for the people she served and felt that she did not truly want to quit. Jenny decided that she needed to visit Sally. Once she arrived at this young, single missionary's home, Jenny knew immediately what the problem was. Sally had nothing in her home except a bed and a minimal number of essentials. Sally's home was not a home at all. She was not living in her space, she was simply occupying it.

Immediately, Jenny went shopping and purchased some pretty, yet modest items to decorate Sally's home: colorful wall coverings, pillows, and lovely rugs. After a small, meaningful transformation of the space, the most amazing thing happened—Sally decided to stay. By Jenny helping Sally to see the value of her home, she stayed and continued to serve with joy! The key is to value yourself and your home, even if you are the only one who lives there.

Faith for Contentment

Whether you are single, widowed, or living with a large family, your home is important. So, whatever station of life you are in, give value and attention to your home. I have a love for widows and we have a strong group of women in our church that call themselves W.O.W. which means, "Women of Worth." I have watched in awe, as they continue to grow and add value to their lives by being a blessing to others. Joy and contentment are tangible in their lives.

1 Timothy 6:6 says, "Godliness accompanied with contentment (that contentment which is a sense of inward sufficiency) is great and abundant gain" (AMP). Even though these women are widows, they still seek to add value to their homes and relationships. The simple act of having friends over for tea can add value to yourself and to those you include.

Are you a person of joy and contentment? Sometimes I think that as modern women we feel the need to complicate our lives with unnecessary "to-do-lists" and endless efforts to prove our significance

> You can make your home and relationships all they can be through faith and connection.

through volunteering and busyness. But while it is important to devote ourselves to worthy causes, it is equally important not to become out of balance. Yes, service is important, but it is also important to pray about each opportunity that comes your way before you say yes.

Ask God to show you where to direct your passion and energy. Honor and value must start with us—knowing who we truly are in

Christ. Married or not, honor and value yourself as the daughter that you are of the King of Kings!

Faith for Value

I have a heart for mentorship and find great joy in training and teaching young women. Years ago, I was mentoring a young single mom and we were working on her budget. She had a young daughter and was struggling to make ends meet, however, she was very passionate about rescuing dogs and was spending five hundred dollars each month towards this cause. While I understand what it is like to love animals, it is essential that everything is in proper alignment in our lives.

For example, for this devoted young mom, she was unknowingly giving more value and honor to animals than she was giving to herself and to her daughter. It was difficult for her to walk away from her passion, but after she and I openly discussed the importance of priorities, she knew it was the right thing to do. She was trying to add value to her life by rescuing dogs, however, this was giving her a false sense of significance. She was all she needed to be. After walking in honesty, God began to bless her with new passions and opened doors for her in ways that were in alignment with her priorities.

I have another dear friend who also adores dogs and would even make diapers for them. She already had two very cute little doggies, but she wanted a dog that she could take on walks and that would encourage her to exercise. On Mother's Day, she called me to announce with great excitement that she had a new addition, Trapper John.

Time passed, and I began to notice that each time I called her our conversation would often be interrupted, as she was yelling at her beloved Trapper John. Inevitably, our call would abruptly end with something like, "Uh oh...I got-ta go!" She was not getting any sleep due to the dog's behavior and she was becoming more miserable with each passing day. Like any dog lover would do, she hired a dog trainer to help. This went on for months.

One day, she and I met for a dinner-date and I noticed how tired and worn she looked. I asked, "How is it going with Trapper John?" She replied, "Well, I caught him on top of the dining table eating an avocado...seeds and all. If only I could get him under control." I could tell that this situation was breaking her heart. I looked at my friend and, taking her by the hand, I said "Pam, you will still go to heaven if you get rid of that dog!" She went right home and the next day, found Trapper John a more suitable home. You may love dogs or pets just as much as my dear friend Pam, but honestly evaluate and thoughtfully consider what the influence of a pet means for your relationships and daily life.

When my children were young I greatly desired for them to experience farm life in the same way that I had, so to our home we added a rabbit, fish, dog, goat and for a small time a mini horse. This was my way of trying to give my girls what I thought was a better life—but I was simply filling it with stuff.

I did not realize it at the time, but what my children really needed was their mom not being stressed out over Nannie the goat running away, wondering who was going to feed Bugsy the rabbit, or Rajah the dog being depressed. For real—the dog was sad. I think it is safe to say that I did not "ponder much about life clutter" back then. Hindsight is always 20/20!

Pause and Ponder

Let's take a minute and do just that—let's "pause and ponder." We talked about imagining our husbands dressed in the color yellow, but what if I asked you to imagine your day bathed in yellow—the rainbow's brightest color. What would a "Yellow-Day" look like for you?

A "Yellow-Day" for me: seeing all three of my daughters on the same day, time with my Honey Bun (one of my pet names for Terry!), enjoying an event with my grandchildren and it goes smoothly, eating at a restaurant that has tablecloths, and visiting someone in the hospital. Knowing what a "Yellow-Day" looks like for me helps me to be aware and in the moment when I am experiencing this special time and my life feels brighter.

You might have a "Yellow-Day" when you see a butterfly, a blue bird, a sunset or maybe even a rainbow. Write in your journal all of the things that make you feel bright with blessings. Be honest with yourself and keep your list simple as you discover your "Yellow-Day!"

GREEN

Chapter Eight

PEACE IN OUR PRIORITIES

"Green is the prime color of the world, and that from which its loveliness arises."
-Pedro Calderon de la Barca

When God selected the base color for the earth's canvas, He chose green. And green, the primary color in the natural world, is an ideal backdrop. Many of us associate green with life, trees, nature, health and peace. It stimulates feelings of tranquility and rest. Being that green is a combination of both blue and yellow, it is a natural balance of both cool and warm undertones. Also, studies show that the color green helps to alleviate depression, nervousness and anxiety, due to the fact that it is soothing and enhances mental relaxation.

I love what the Psalmist David wrote in Psalms 23:1-2, "The Lord is my shepherd; I have all that I need. He lets me rest in green meadows; He leads me beside peaceful streams" (NLT). God wants to lead us in peace and He wants us to rest in places of peace—in green pastures of life. When I think of the color green, I think of peace, but you cannot have peace apart from priorities. Furthermore, when we are establishing our priorities, we have to be honest with ourselves regarding what God has called us to do versus what we want to do.

Priorities Bring Peace

"Hi ho, hi ho, and it's off to work we go!" Remember these famous lyrics from Snow White and the Seven Dwarfs? In today's world, many of us work outside of our homes, however, for some of us work is home and home is work. Whatever the case may be, finding the balance between work and home can be challenging at best.

Establishing priorities for our lives is essential, no matter where we work or how we give of our time. It can be defined as the giving of our time and attention to what we have deemed as the most important.

In his book, *7 Habits of Highly Effective People*, Stephen Covey writes, "The key is not to prioritize what's on your schedule, but to schedule your priorities."[1] This statement is so true and in order to bring peace to our lives we must first establish priorities, because once we have established our priorities, we will have the courage to say no to the things that don't work.

True Value

It was fall in Texas at the time and I was enjoying a retreat in the hill country. I decided to go for a walk and, as I was meandering through a meadow, I happened to pass by a river. I stopped and, looking down, noticed the smallest frog I had ever seen. This frog was not even an inch long, however, this little frog could hop! I was fascinated by how far it jumped, and I watched as it went 30 to 40 inches at a time. But I also noticed that it was jumping from muck to muck. This tiny frog could travel far greater than its small body should have been able to, however, it continued to land in the mud.

In a similar way, our heavenly Father has made women with great abilities just like that tiny frog. We can stir a pot on the stove with a baby on our hip, while listening to our best friend cry on the phone, all as we tell little John to get down off the table—and not to spill his milk! We can run companies and serve on three different boards. But are these activities defining our value? Are the colors in our lives clearly defined, or are they all dripping together, creating the color of mud?

In his book, *Addicted to Busy*, Pastor Brady Boyd writes, "We are all spread too thin, taking on more than we can handle, trying to do so much—almost as if we are afraid that if we were to take a moment of rest, we might discover that all our Busyness is covering up an essential lack in our lives. But God never meant for us to be so busy. God desires for us to have rest and peace."[2]

I think that believers sometimes try to wear the badge of "I can do all things." But, like the frog, are we leaping into mud through our multi-tasking and our busyness? Where are we landing as we leap through life? We must be brave enough to assess our lives with openness and honesty. And ceasing to multi-task is an important step in the direction of peace and priorities.

To have peace in our lives we must have clearly defined priorities, however, what does peace look like exactly? You may be thinking that peace is a cool and calm feeling. Or, perhaps you imagine peace as a quiet house while the kids are at school.

While there may be many ways to define peace, I feel that it is important to note what the Bible has to say about peace. The prophet Isaiah writes, "For thus says the Lord: Behold, I will extend peace to her like a river, and the glory of the nations like an overflowing stream" (Isaiah 66:12a, AMP). He goes on further to declare in Isaiah 48:17–18, "Thus says the Lord, your Redeemer, the Holy One of Israel: I am the Lord your God, Who teaches you to profit, who leads you in the way that you should go. Oh, that you had hearkened to my commandments! Then your peace and prosperity would have been like a flowing river" (AMP).

Learning how to cultivate the fruit of peace in our ever-changing world may seem overwhelming—life just never seems to stop. Some may think, "If I can just simplify my life, I'll have peace. Or, let me just eliminate some people from my life and I will have peace!" But while life is always in motion like the ocean or a river, true peace is not obtained through our human intellect. Personally, I always wanted peace like a pond. I thought if I could get things to "work-out," I would feel peaceful. Big news flash! Peace is an inside job.

In Matthew 8:23–26, Jesus and His disciples were in a boat when a storm arose. Jesus was asleep: He had peace. I wonder how long the disciples waited before they awakened Jesus. How long did they try to ride out the storm? Were they throwing things overboard to lighten their load—simplifying their lives?

My friend, no matter what you're going through, Jesus is there with you! He is in your boat right now! Wake Him up! Sometimes prayer is the last thing we do after trying to handle the storm, yet

Jesus wants to be our deliverer and our redeemer—the One who calms the storm.

Philippians 4:6–7 says, "Don't worry about anything; instead, pray about everything. Tell God what you need and thank Him for all he has done. Then you will experience God's peace, which exceeds anything we can understand. His peace will guard your hearts and minds as you live in Christ Jesus" (NLT). True peace only comes from the value of knowing who we are in Jesus and that He is always with us—calming our chaos.

The Multi-Tasking Myth

Peace is not the result of "simplify, simplify," as Thoreau once wrote. However, peace is the absence of multi-tasking. That's why I want to talk about a few beliefs that erode our peace. Many of us have surmised that multi-tasking is advantageous, but recent studies of the brain attest otherwise.

Dr. Caroline Leaf is a cognitive neuroscientist with a PhD in Communication Pathology, specializing in Neuropsychology. Regarding multi-tasking she writes: "It is actually impossible to multitask. We don't do multiple things at once; we actually shift between different tasks quickly. If we do this well, we are doing busy well. But, if we are doing busy badly, we are doing what I call milkshake multitasking. We cause literal neurochemical chaos in our brain, which, in turn, causes literal brain damage...Multi-tasking is a myth. Paying attention to one task at a time is the correct way."3

It is impossible for the brain to do two tasks at once! Yet not only is multi-tasking scientifically impossible, it can also be dangerous. I had a friend who had a list of exercises that she claimed could be done while driving. I tried them—only once. I felt defeated. I wondered how she could do this and I couldn't.

Presently, there is a multi-tasking that is truly taking lives: texting and driving. I am sure we could list many more dangerous side-effects of multi-tasking. The point is that trying to prioritize too many tasks at once is not prioritizing at all. We must endeavor to focus on one task at a time, taking all our needs to Jesus—the captain of our boat. Wake Him up!

In addition to multi-tasking, there is another villain in our picture of peace and it strives to rob our value of self. It sounds like this: "I should." The list you may find yourself saying if you are facing the leviathan of "should" says: "Maybe I should quit work? Maybe I should go back to school? Maybe I should serve in that ministry? Maybe I should do more...of something?" Oh the "Shame game" we play that steals our peace. Do you find that this conversation is much too familiar?

There is an old song titled, "He Pilots my Ship" that says: "I won't sail these stormy seas no more lest Jesus leads the way, I won't ever drift so far from the shore that I can't hear what He has to say. For I belong to a fleet that's sailing today on a glorious one-way trip. We'll land safely on shore to sail no more, Oh Jesus pilots my ship."4 No matter where you're at in your life, it is never too late to commit your way to the Lord, letting Him sail your ship to green pastures.

Pause and Ponder

We are going to "Pause and Ponder" a bit early in this chapter. Find a cozy place to sit and grab your journal and Bible. Before you begin, quiet yourself before the Lord. Once you've found a place of peace, read the following passage from Psalms aloud. Let each word wash over you, cleansing you: "I wait quietly before God, for my victory comes from him. He alone is my rock and my salvation, my fortress where I will never be shaken...Let all that I am wait quietly before God, for my hope is in him. He alone is my rock and my salvation, my fortress where I will not be shaken. My victory and honor come from God alone. He is my refuge, a rock where no enemy can reach me. O my people, trust in him at all times. Pour out your heart to him, for God is our refuge" Psalms 62:1, 2, 5–8 (NLT). "Commit everything you do to the Lord. Trust him, and he will help you. He will make your innocence radiate like the dawn, and the justice of your cause will shine like the noonday sun. Be still in the presence of the Lord and wait patiently for him to act." Psalms 37:5–7a (NLT).

Write in your journal all the decisions you are presently making, all the "should do's." Now, pray over this list, working through each item with true hearing and honesty. Some things may be on your list to impress others, yet they have no value. Other things on your list may bring value to your family and your lifestyle. Some things on your list may be there because you simply find great joy in doing them like your career. Name the value that each one of your choices brings. For example: "I find value in my decision to..." Keep this list accessible and re-evaluate your list each year.

By being honest with yourself regarding your priorities, you will now be able to assess your list with confidence knowing: I add value to my life by bringing in income, I add value to my family by home schooling, or I add value to my life and others by leading a small group. As we become stronger and more confident with the direction of our lives, we will be able to embrace our fellow sisters without jealousy.

In her book, *Women at War*, Jan Greenwood tells the story of how she used to ride her yellow, mini-bike with the wind in her hair, while singing at the top of her lungs, "I am women hear me roar!"5 At Gateway Church, where I attend, Pastor Debbie Morris oversees our women's ministry and she can roar, but I must say she does so in a sweet, yet powerful tone because her priorities have been established. She is a woman of peace, and she is able to empower other women to find peace and value with who they are. Likewise, your list of what you value provides you with priority and purpose.

"First keep peace with yourself, then you can also bring peace to others." –Thomas a Kempis

I have discovered that my day is more peaceful with a to-do list.

By approaching my day one item at a time, I am able to stay out of the mud. Just be sure to create a daily list that can be revised throughout your day as needs arise or as you have issues to address. As a business woman, I have many clients, all with design needs, and it is important for me to be able to reprioritize throughout my day. However, having focus brings value and peace to my work. If it is worth doing, it is worth doing well!

Whether you work in or out of your home, making a list of priorities that ensures your focus is a matter of valuing yourself, and will empower you to find peace even in the simplest of tasks.

Value Your Personhood

As women, we must know the value of prioritizing not only self-care but also the care of our spirit and soul. While many of us may find it comfortable to discuss how we will prioritize our families or our careers, many women struggle with finding peace in the priority of self-care. But it's important to realize that no one is going to make you a priority but you. No one is going to say, "Get some rest. Get your nails done. Eat right and please go get your hair done!"

Women sometimes wrestle with creating balance in their lives. For example, finding peace to simply take time for a bubble bath is often not given value, however, by simply prioritizing 20 minutes a day for activities that you enjoy or that you find rejuvenating, you will be prioritizing a sense of self-value—treasuring your personhood.

In order to give value to yourself, you must make time for essentials like prayer and scripture meditation, adequate sleep, exercise, and even the occasional massage and bubble bath. King David writes in Psalm 23:2a, "He makes me to lie down in green pastures" (NKJV).

"Green pastures" in this passage is speaking of pastures consisting of tender, green grass, signifying how God not only wants to deal tenderly with us but He also wants us to deal tenderly with ourselves. God's desire for us, His daughters, is for us to rest in tender green places, where there is life and health, but for this to happen we have to be in agreement with Him.

The sheep could stubbornly stay standing in the green pastures, "Baaing" at the shepherd that they are "just fine" and argue that they do not need to lay down. Or, the sheep could receive the shepherd's tender care and lay down in the pastures of tenderness. I don't know about you, but I want to rest in God's tenderness of green: peace.

Not only do we need to be tender with ourselves, we also need to make time for activities that refresh us. This will look differently for everyone and, like defining your personal style, you may need to define what rejuvenates you. For example, does taking a walk restore you or sharing a cup of tea with a friend? What about seeing a movie or having lunch somewhere new?

Quiet yourself and ponder the times that you have truly felt at peace or refreshed—personally restored. What were you doing? Who were you doing it with? Make a list that you can refer to of the activities that refresh you or the things you find restful. To your list, you may also want to include time for reading a good book. Studies show that reading, especially a narrative fiction, helps to alleviate stress and enhance a sense of belonging, all of which are essential for personal wholeness and health. Be sure to prioritize yourself in a way that makes you feel beautiful.

Green for Style

In addition to valuing our personhood, there is another task that is common to all women and that is getting dressed! Yet, our ever-changing couture can cause us to feel overwhelmed as we strive to look our best. If your office is in your home or you care for someone in your home, it adds value if you get dressed each morning, as if you were going somewhere. I am not a fashion expert, but as a professional that deals with décor, it is important that I meet my clients looking as though I know how to color coordinate!

I am sure that we all have a funny fashion story, but mine is truly funny even though at the time I was mortified! I was 16 years old and there was a dance at our school. I had been taking guitar lessons from a young man who worked at our local music store (I still can't play the guitar), and my guitar teacher was 16 and well—need I say more. He also played in a band and I had talked the principal of our school into letting his group play for our dance. Sadly, this meant that I wouldn't be dancing, but I didn't care. The excitement of going was more than my heart could take.

My mom took me shopping and there on the rack was the dress of my dreams! It was a long, maxi-dress in a pink-print cotton. It had puff sleeves and a lace collar with buttons that went all the way down the front and was finished off with a pink ribbon belt. Oddly, it was the only one on the rack and it happened to be in my size. I loved the dress and my mom loved the price! I felt beautiful as I wore my long, flowing, pink dress to the dance, and I had a great time watching my guitar teacher play. I even received my first kiss and home I went.

As I was hanging up my dress, something caught my eye that I hadn't noticed before. On the tag of the dress were letters that spelled out a word—robe! I let out a scream and my mom came running, thinking that I was either dying or a stranger had broken into our home. It took some time to calm me down so that I could explain to my mom that I had just worn a robe to the school dance!

Don't Worry About It

The last thing we need to be stressed about is getting dressed, but how in this age of "Fashionista" do we find peace in what to wear? The Bible says a few things regarding this topic. In Matthew 6:31, Jesus said, "Don't worry about what you will wear." Yet Jesus Himself wore such a nice robe that it was gambled for. I sometimes think about the man who won it; he must have been so glad to win such a fine robe, but did he ever wear it? How did he feel when he looked in his closet and saw it hanging there? Maybe we can see what happened to him one day on one of those "Heavenly—DVDs."

Not thinking about what to wear sounds hard to do, but I have some ideas that help me and may be of benefit to you. First, I believe it's important to understand the difference between styles and trends. Women with style are distinctive and they don't go too far left or right, but simply look well-tailored. Today, our best example of this would be Kate Middleton, Prince William's wife.

If you look in any magazine, you will quickly notice the list of the seasons' "must-haves" or the latest trend, but we first must have value in who we are, not in the next trend we purchase. It's important to know your clothing style, just like you know your home style. Also, know what colors and cuts look best on your shape. This will change how you shop.

Personally, I love fall colors, but I look best in black and white, pretty pinks, berry-red colors and some blues and grays, so I can look at the top of a rack and know whether or not it is for me. However, I have a red-headed friend who looks fabulous when she wears yellows, gold, olives and all my favorite fall colors. There is so much information on how to find the style and colors that are right for you, and it's worth taking the time to develop this knowledge.

For instance, I know that upright collars give the appearance of a long neck. Soft-light colors near one's face is a friend for the aging. And solid colored outfits appear powerful. Queen Elizabeth II can mostly be seen wearing a solid colored outfit. When you think about Jackie Kennedy, Princess Grace, and Audrey Hepburn, in addition to the top fashion ladies of our day, you will see that they stay true to a style and not a trend. Coco Chanel once said, "Fashion fades, only style remains the same."

If you find this process difficult, ask a stylist for help, keeping in mind this is not to be a legalistic idea of "You can't wear a trend." Just don't anchor your wardrobe around a trend. Instead, let your wardrobe be anchored by your distinctive style.

Stepping into the Wardrobe

"Building a proper wardrobe is like building a home. Indeed, you should think of it like a home, because it is something you're going to live in. It must be comfortable and suit all your needs."
–Edith Head

The idea of a wardrobe is distinct from just having clothes. For example, you should be able to walk into your closet right now and find something to wear for a wedding, luncheon, funeral, Sunday service or picnic. As a young girl, I remember my mom's funeral outfit. She always wore the same one. It was a lovely, classic black dress with a scalloped collar. She had a matching hat that was a black ring with a small veil. I loved it when my mom went to a funeral simply because I thought she always looked stunning. She had acquired the pieces needed for a functioning wardrobe and it served her well.

For some, however, building a wardrobe can be overwhelming. If you are not sure what works for you, ask a friend that looks put together—she'll be glad to help, I'm sure! Personally, I have a yearly budget that I divide into four parts: one for each season. I have four shopping trips a year and I go with purpose—like a grocery store trip with a list. If my closet needs shoes or a great pair of jeans, then that is what I look for. But if I want a designer bag, I may end up only buying a bag that season. This helps me to prioritize and budget. Further, it encourages me to be more particular when I'm shopping.

When you make purchases not based on the latest sale or shoe style, you will have a wardrobe that meets your needs and you will wear your clothes much longer.

Deciding What to Wear

Recently, I read a study that we only wear 20% of our clothing

80% of the time. I think that is wasteful. While I do not have the best-looking wardrobe, it serves me well. I have developed a fun system that enables me to not only have more variety in what I wear each day (making me look like I have more outfits than I really do), but my system also helps me utilize my wardrobe to its highest potential.

Because I see my clients repeatedly, it is important to me to have on a unique outfit each time, thus I have chosen to hang all my clothes (I don't like folding and this works for me). I hang all my pants together, all my shirts together, all my dresses together and so on (you get the picture). I even hang my scarves!

I select one piece to start off my outfit. So, for Monday, whichever item is hanging first in my queue for my dress and skirts is what I wear. Then I select whatever else I need to go with it. This is just like if you had a pillow or a throw rug that you loved, and you designed your room around it. If I find an item I don't like or it's not a good fit, I simply put it in the bag I keep handy and move to the next piece.

On Tuesday, it's pants day, however, if there are a pair of jeans hanging and I don't need to be in jeans that day, then I will simply skip over the jeans and choose the next item in my line-up. Jackets start on Wednesday and on it goes!

For the weekend, I choose anything I feel like. This allows me to create new looks all the time and edit my wardrobe continuously. This may not be the way you would want to organize your wardrobe, but it works for me. Just remember, only purchase clothing that you love and be particular when you shop. When you do this, you will always look great! Dressing each morning is important no matter what your day's priorities are. I have a wardrobe adventure every morning. I look forward to getting dressed each day and you can too!

Dressed for Success

How you get dressed each day is significant. When you dress

with purpose and priority, you will be more energized and more willing to embrace the day's challenges. Likewise, when you are dressed nicely, it helps to boost your confidence and overall sense of self-value.

I love what author and success coach Stacia Pierce has to say on the topic of dressing for success: "Beautify yourself and upgrade your personal image." When you look good, you feel good. Even if you work from a home office, dress to impress at your desk. Get up every day and dress as though you have important business meetings to attend, even if they are just conference calls you'll be taking at your desk. You'll find it much easier to meet new people, express yourself, present in meetings and close the deal when you are looking and feeling your best.

When the Bible says to be ready in season and out of season, I feel this can apply to getting dressed each day. I used to carpool my two oldest daughters and their friends to school and I always dressed very nice for the day. One day (when there were no cell-phones), I told my husband that I would be visiting the new grocery store after I dropped off the kids. The store was offering a free carton of eggs and I wanted mine!

I was at the store with a cart-full of food and my baby girl in tow when my name was called over the intercom. I went to the front of the store and they handed me the phone whereupon I discovered that my father-in-law had just passed away. I left my cart (yes, I did get my eggs) and I quickly picked up my girls and was able to be there for my family. I was already dressed nicely, so I was ready for whatever was going to come my way. It takes just as much time to put on a pair of jeans and a cute top, as it does to throw on sweats and a t-shirt. Value yourself by finding peace with prioritizing you!

Live in Color

I loved the late Zig Ziglar. At the age of 19, I attended his "Richer Life" seminar where I spent four days learning many of his positive thinking techniques. I was fascinated by one story in particular, regarding his wife. He said, "I love the day of the week when that red-head that I love so much gets her hair done." Zig shared, "I enjoy the company of that red-head the most, when she feels like a million dollars. When she feels her best, I know she will be at her best."

The worth of a woman has nothing to do with what house she lives in or what car she drives. The bigger question is, "How do you feel about yourself?" Embrace truth regarding your identity and let the truth set you free. You are beautiful and wonderfully made!

When you dress with purpose and priority, you will be more energized and more willing to embrace the day's challenges.

Personally, I have always dreamed in color—I live in color—color defines me. I realized early in life that I think a little different than most and my eyes see the world a little different, because of this, it took me awhile to find value in the way God made me. In fact, at one point in my life, I was very co-dependent—always looking outside myself to find value.

Today, I know that I am perfect in my heavenly Father's eyes, and I know that it is okay to be me. Likewise, you are designed by God to be you—embrace it!

"The Beauty of a Woman" By Audrey Hepburn

The Beauty of a woman is not in
The clothes she wears,
The figure that she carries, or the
Way she combs her hair.
The Beauty of a woman must be
Seen from in her eyes,
Because that is the doorway to
Her heart, the place where love
Resides.
The Beauty of a women is not in
A facial mole,
But true beauty in a woman is
Reflected in her soul.
It is the caring that she lovingly gives,
The passion that she shows,
And the beauty of a woman
With passing years only grows.

Pause and Ponder

Grab your journal and write down a dollar amount you think would represent your worth. Now, make a list of three friends you will call to ask them your value. "How much am I worth?" Get a dollar amount. Tell them you are just working on your value and self-worth. Their amounts will be higher than yours, I am sure! Are you a million-dollar girl or five and a dime? When was the last time you went for a walk, took a bubble bath or had your nails done? Invest in the bank called "You" and bring the value of green to your personhood!

Now I think we need to take a field trip. Go to your closet right now and ask yourself: Is this working for me? Have I built a wardrobe or have I just accumulated clothing? How can I have a wardrobe that meets my needs? What are my needs? Are the colors in my closet right for me? Do I even like what I see? Be prepared to part with some things. List your clothing priorities and what type of wardrobe best suits your lifestyle.

Peace from Work to Home

"Strength and honor are her clothing; she shall rejoice in time to come...She watches over the ways of her household and does not eat the bread of idleness."
Proverbs 31:25, 27 (NKJV)

Everyone is hard at work in the world that we live today, and the lines between work and home have been permanently obscured. After-hour emails and clients that have our cell phone numbers can cause us to have to walk a tight-rope of connectivity, leaving us suspended over a chasm of disconnection.

But, as we color and clearly define our lives, it's important to make the distinction between work and home. Yet, for many, work and home are one and the same. Because of this, it's natural to wonder how we can best disconnect from work and prioritize connecting with our home. A good place to start might be through engaging your senses. For instance, when you are ready to make the home connection, say aloud, "I'm home!" Even if no one hears you, your senses will be engaged that a change or shift is taking place.

I use an apron to do the trick. I try to walk in the door and put on my apron at the end of each work day. Even if I happen to be working from my home office that day, I still go through the same routine because it helps my mind make the transition from a "work" mindset to a "home" mindset, thus, for me the connection is made, the colors are clear, and my life is more defined. My apron routine connects me with my kitchen and my family who know I will be preparing something because we value connection, and for us connection happens around the dinner table.

I have realized, however, that I must respect others and myself—being mindful of the time and the home zone. Perhaps you might strategize a routine that will enable you to completely be in the moment: connecting with your home and hearth. The word hearth literally means the floor of a fireplace and is the area that gathers the most heat. It symbolizes one's home because it is the place that warms us and comforts us—a place of connection for our hearts. We need to make connection with our homes a priority. So, consider having a routine that includes lighting a candle and turning on music once you are home or, if you are like me, throw on an apron.

Truly, reconnecting with your space and disconnecting from your day is the essence of domestic synergy. Because of this, if you are a stay-at-home mom, it may be good to plan a transition time an hour before your husband arrives home. Instruct the children to begin putting away their toys in preparation for the evening and for "Home-Connection."

The apron project will change your family's perspective, not only their view of you, but you will also feel empowered. The apron is like a flag waving to your family, "I'm serving you." For me, throwing on an apron allows me to work in the kitchen without needing to change clothes. I may change my shoes, but then, "I'm good to go!" I am able, as the evening unwinds, to connect with my family—the ones that I value most. Today, begin planning ways to connect with your home.

In addition to connecting with our homes once our day's work is complete, it's also important to know how to guide that sacred connection time. For instance, in the age of technology in which we currently live, it is important to set clear boundaries on all electronics. We need to steward technology, not be ruled by it.

Personally, I hate conflict, however, I have learned that sometimes in order to have peace, you must face a few battles. One of the battles worth facing is the battle of no-technology or cell phones at the dinner table. I decided a long time ago that no one is allowed to play a video game at dinner. You might experience great resistance over this rule, however, the long-term benefits of connection will be worth the price. The more you value your priority to have dinner together and spend quality family time together, the more you will be willing to fight for it.

I had a season when our grandchildren shared our home. I enjoyed watching my sweet granddaughter and energetic grandson change dispositions at the table as they responded to my expectation of sitting still and being fully present. Once upon a time, my grandson would eat in two minutes and then want to get down to go play, but now he doesn't ask to go play because he is engaged in conversation. The other night we were all enjoying him telling us story after story.

Just remember your actions speak louder than words. For example, if your children see you are disconnecting from technology and cell phones to engage in table time, they will do so as well. And the same applies with friends. In a kind tone, let them know, "I so want to spend this short hour with you. Do you mind if we put our phones away?"

Peace in the Priority of Rest

"On the seventh day God had finished his work of creation, so he rested from all his work. And God blessed the seventh day and declared it holy, because it was the day when he rested from all his work of creation."
Genesis 2:2–3 (NLT)

A few days after God said, "Let there be light," we read that on the seventh day, "He rested from all his work." Sometimes I wonder: are we resting or testing? God rested on the seventh day, but not because He was tired. I think He rested so that He could enjoy the creation that He, the great Designer, had made. God was demonstrating for us how to disconnect and take a Sabbath. In the same way, we need to show those we love how to do the same thing: leading by example into places of rest.

Dr. Brené Brown writes in her book, *The Gifts of Imperfection*, how she believes perfection to be mythical, stating: "Perfectionism is a self-destructive and addictive belief system that fuels this primary thought: 'If I look perfect, and do everything perfectly, I can avoid or minimize the painful feelings of shame, judgment, and blame.' Understanding the difference between healthy striving and perfectionism is critical to laying down the shield and picking up your life. Research shows that perfectionism hampers success. In fact, it's often the path to depression, anxiety, addiction, and life paralysis."[7]

Like my girls matching socks and hair-bows, my perfectionism was just a cover-up for what I was wrestling with inside. In order to truly prioritize "green" in our lives, we must first discover what brings us rest and peace. So, value yourself enough to lay aside perfection and to rest in "green" pastures of grace and mercy— God's perfection.

Psalms 46:10a states, "Be still, and know that I am God" (NIV). Psalm 100:3 also says, "Know that the LORD is God. It is he who made us, and we are his; we are his people, the sheep of his pasture" (NIV). God wants to be our good Shepherd and He wants us to rest in tender pastures. Regarding these verses from Psalms, ask yourself: "What does a day of rest look like for me? How would I design a perfect day of rest?"

Be intentional in the process of answering those questions. You may even notice, because you will be starting from a place of rest, that the remainder of your week is more productive. So, flunk the test and rest!

Peace in the Money

Finally, I believe we cannot fully have the "green" of peace and priority in our lives, unless we also have peace and priority in our finances. So, we need to talk money—you know that green stuff in your wallet.

Pastor Robert Morris is known for his teachings based on his life and book, *The Blessed Life*. He believes that not only should we want to be people who are living to give, but we must also be living below our means in order to have peace in our finances. In addition to Pastor Robert Morris's teachings, Dave Ramsey has also created Financial Peace University, which teaches practical biblical steps in order to help individuals achieve peace in their finances. Proverbs 22:17 states, "Incline your ear and hear the words of the wise and apply your mind to my knowledge" (NASB).

Pastor Robert shares that money has a spirit (the spirit of mammon) and he explains, as it pertains to money, how we may have thoughts of greed or we may even be overly troubled and consumed regarding money that we can think of nothing else: assailed by worry and anxiety—financially dysfunctional.

After Terry's illness, years ago, I realized how clueless I was regarding the finances in our home. From one woman to another, I implore you, please familiarize yourself with the financial situation in your home. Find peace with relating to your finances and become accustomed to how bills are paid and what the processes are. This is a part of valuing yourself. No one plans to be without your spouse, but once Terry was ill, I realized how unprepared I truly was to handle our finances at that time.

Providing for your family is a high priority and having peace in this area of your life is a blessing. The other day, my two grandchildren, Marley (five) and Devon (six), were sitting in my kitchen while I was serving them chocolate cake. I said, in regard to the cake, "This is rich!" Devon looked up at Marley, and asked, "Do you know what rich means?" Marley replied, "It means you're lucky!" Well, luck is not exactly what we are talking about but know who you are and the state of your finances. Discover the peace that passes all understanding which comes from asking the Prince of Peace to take control not only of your finances but every area of your life.

Pause and Ponder

Now, let's take a moment to ponder on peace. Green is at the center of our rainbow, and peace can be the centerpiece of your life. If you mixed all the seven colors of the rainbow, you would have the color of mud; and yet, the Designer of your life wants to clearly define all the colors of your Rainbow, so let Him.

God desires for you to have peace in the priority of family, marriage, and relationships; to have peace in the priority of self-care and the care of others; and to have peace in your finances. All we have to do is just ask, and He will cause you to begin leaping through green pastures. No more jumping in the mud—unless it is for fun! He is waiting to paint your life canvas with clearly defined beauty and peace.

BLUE

Chapter Nine

BEING HUNGRY FOR

HOSPITALITY

"If you really want to make a friend, go to someone's house and eat with him...the people who give you their food give you their heart." — Cesar Chavez

Did you ever play the game Hungry Hippos when you were a kid? I did, and it was always a lot of fun. I remember my family and I would place a bunch of marbles in the center of the board and energetically open and close the mouths of our hippos, gobbling up the marbles as fast as we could. Well, in the same way those hippos are hungry for marbles, our homes are hungry for hospitality.

On any given day in my childhood home, my dad would show up with someone in need or someone with whom he desired to share hospitality. He had a big heart and he would often bring home people or families he had picked up from the roadside. One year, my mom's sister (who was newly widowed) and her two small girls lived in our home. We were always having guests over—our home served others.

The Apostle Paul writes in Hebrews, "Don't neglect to show hospitality to strangers, for thereby some have entertained angels unawares" Hebrews 13:2 (ESV). I don't know if we ever entertained angels, but I do know that God wants us to have a spirit of hospitality in our homes. And my dad displayed this spirit very well.

According to Merriam-Webster's Dictionary, hospitality means: "generous and friendly treatment of visitors, the activity of providing food and drinks, etc. for people who are guests." Oxford Dictionary explains it as: "the friendly and generous reception and entertainment of guests, visitors or strangers." In light of Hebrews 13:2, I like how this definition includes the reception of strangers. Interestingly, the word, "hospitality" comes from the Latin word, hospitalitas, which is where we get our word for hospital.

God desires that our homes be places of spiritual and emotional healing and restoration, as we invite the rainbow's beloved color blue into our homes—the color of hospitality.

To me, blue represents hospitality because blue is a spiritual color that is nostalgic in nature. It is the color of the sky and reflected in the ocean, thus it is cooling and calming. Many see blue as being trustworthy, dependable and committed—a constant in our lives. Further, the color blue causes the body to produce chemicals that are calming, producing a restful state of mind. In the Chinese culture, blue is the color of spring—when new life is birthed. In the Aztec culture, blue symbolizes sacrifice.

I find both of these examples enlightening because the idea here is that hospitality, just like spring, is to be life-giving—ever new and always welcoming new guests. But just like blue is the color of sacrifice for the Aztecs, hospitality often does require us to lay down our own desires for the sake of others. And if we want our homes to be places of healing—places of spring—we must fill our homes with the color blue, the life-giving spirit of hospitality.

Pause and Ponder

Before we go any further, let's take a moment to "Pause and Ponder." Go get your journal and show yourself some hospitality by grabbing some tea or coffee in your favorite mug or tea cup. When you read the word "hospitality" what are some of the first thoughts that leap into your mind? Write them down. Do you already have the color blue of hospitality in your home? If so, how do you feel you could increase blue's influence?

The simple acts of cooking, cleaning, food shopping, and feeding people in our home are tasks that can simply feel like chores; however, know there is a difference between hospitality and just eating. Hospitality is the act of dining with emotion and inviting others to share in the enriching experience. Further, hospitable dining is the element of connection, where there is time for more than just putting food into our mouths. It allows for individual spirits to connect while a sense of belonging is cultivated.

Yes, we all have to eat, but how we eat has the potential to create treasured memories and improved health.

The Chef's Hat

Author, Virginia Woolf, once wrote, "One cannot think well, love well, or sleep well, if one has not dined well." Like artistic design, cooking is something that can be learned and mastered. Chef Wolfgang Puck said, "Cooking is like painting or writing a song. Just as there are only so many notes or colors, there are only so many flavors. It's how you combine them that sets you apart." Yet while cooking is an art, it is also a craft. And, like any craft, it must be learned.

In the same way that you may have learned a few ways to tie your shoe or fix your hair, I think everyone should learn how to cook a dish or two. There are one hundred small pleats in a chef's hat and they stand for one hundred ways to cook an egg. Now, I am not suggesting you learn the one hundred ways to cook an egg, but I think learning three wouldn't hurt!

Many women find it increasingly difficult to make friends with their kitchen (making the connection). But I have found that if you capture the heartbeat of your kitchen, you will discover a treasure trove of food memories awaiting you and your loved ones. Cooking doesn't have to be hard, and if you keep in mind the goal of cooking—to create hospitality in your home and create memories—learning to cook will feel like a labor of love.

By learning a few simple dishes, you will begin to build a connection with your kitchen and confidence in your cooking. And, in addition to learning a few simple meals, learning how to make homemade sauces and soups will take your cooking to a whole new level!

Now, at this point you may be thinking, "Deb, I hate to cook!" But I'm not asking you to cook for the sake of cooking. I'm asking you to create memories and connections with those you love. I'm asking you to create an experience that will stay with your friends and family for years to come. It will be like a lighthouse drawing them back to your table.

I want you to capture the essence of the color blue. We cannot have the rainbow without it, and we cannot have hospitality without food and the preparations that go along with it. So, if you don't like to cook, just picture yourself as a mood and memories creator, one who makes a nostalgic experience for those you love. Think of yourself like a fire-maker, creating a warm place where others will come to warm their hands and their hearts.

I Want Fish!

By now, you probably get the picture that my dad's parenting philosophy was to throw me into the deep-end and watch me swim. There's one memory in particular that comes to mind during the summer before I turned 11. My family and I were still living on our farm in Ohio and my mom had just opened Billie's Health Food Store. It was a busy time for our family, and my dad decided it was time for me to start cooking. I never questioned my dad. If he thought I could cook, then I would cook.

Because of this, cooking adventures began for me at an early age and started out of necessity. There was the cake I made with salt (not sugar), and there was the spaghetti dinner when the spaghetti was all stuck together. It poured out of the bowl in one big glob (later, Mom explained that I needed to rinse the noodles after cooking).

Yet, in spite of these childhood culinary masterpieces, I will never forget the day my dad called home and informed me that he wanted fish for dinner. "But daddy, I don't know how to cook fish!" I tried to explain. His retort, "Then learn!" And he hung up the phone. So, I learned. I began to teach myself how to cook by reading cookbooks and anything else I could find on the topic of cooking. I even read the entire contents information on a box of baking soda, which served me well.

One day, my Mamaw was visiting. Now, you could say her life motto was, "waste not, want not." She would save aluminum foil and rinse plastic-bags for re-use. She would even place her Crisco containers on top of the gas stove so that she could slowly melt the contents, thus allowing her to waste nothing.

Well, one day, Mamaw had forgotten to get all the paper off the side of the Crisco can. So, while it was sitting on the gas stove, the paper caught on fire and the remaining Crisco flamed. The fire was hot and high, and we didn't have a fire extinguisher. I then grabbed a box of baking soda and threw it at the fire. White powder flumed in the air and out went the flames.

Mom and Mamaw stood in the kitchen with their mouths hanging open. I was just as surprised as they were that it worked, and, to this day, I keep a box of baking soda near my stove (I tell my girls to do the same).

My dad's philosophy of "just learn," has never left me. And my desire is that you will have learned how to cook a few new dishes and will have experienced some new cooking adventures too before you finish this book!

Food Memories

I have many wonderful "food memories" from my youth. I call them "food memories" because my family knew the value of dining and hospitality. My parents and grandparents knew that mealtime was an opportunity to create long-lasting memories that would continue to warm our hearts and welcome us home for years to come.

I was blessed to have two grandmothers, both of whom were very dear to me. One of my grandmothers was from Kentucky, the other from Louisiana. One said: breakfast, lunch, and dinner, while the other grandmother said: breakfast, dinner, and supper.

My southern grandmother always set the table with all the food and served the plates at the table. Today, she is in her 90's and still sets her table and serves the food the same way. She likes to cook black-eyed peas, okra, fried flounder, and even squirrel dumplings, serving it all with sweet tea. Her fig preserves and cornbread are not to be missed!

On the farm, my northern grandmother loved to serve fried bologna sandwiches. She would have you sit at the table, then bring you a plate already fixed. She loved to cook wilted greens (fresh garden greens with hot bacon drippings poured on top). I doubt these foods were healthy, but they were certainly delicious!

I'm sure you have food memories of your own. Take a moment to "ponder" how you connect food with loved ones. Maybe your mom had a signature dish or there was an old family recipe that couldn't be left out of any celebration.

What food memories are you creating right now? What type of food memories would you like to leave with your loved ones? These last two questions may be more difficult to answer but they will help as you seek to fill your home with the color of hospitality—blue.

Recipe for Success

Now, you might be reading this and already have cooking down to a fine art. But with fast-food and even faster-paced lives on the rise, it can be easy to feel overwhelmed by it all. You may be thinking, "You really want me to learn to cook in addition to everything else? How will this bring color into my life?"

Personally, I discovered when I was first learning the art of décor that the color blue is the hardest color to decorate with. There are more shades of blue than any other color, and it's the same with cooking. So, where does one begin in such a vast ocean of shades? Begin with your family's favorite dishes.

For example, if your family loves lasagna, have a weekly lasagna night. Every week, create a lasagna and try different recipes. Ask your family to rate each one from one to ten and talk about what they like or don't like, making a notation on your recipe cards so you can remember which one got top ratings. You may even enjoy getting lasagna recipes from friends or family members. On your calendar, write something that says, "Tuesday night is lasagna adventure night" or "lasagna experiment night."

Thinking about it in a fun, new way will help to energize you in this process of discovery. Then, you will discover the recipe your family loves the most. This recipe can become your staple, once-a-week meal that the whole family enjoys.

The key is simple: find what your family loves and make it your own. Personally, I did this with macaroni and cheese. I would make it once a week, trying new recipes, until I created the one my whole family loved and that was the recipe I kept.

My father-in-law made the most delicious white-cream gravy. He tried to teach me several times, but for some reason I wasn't able to prepare it the same way. Mine always turned out lumpy and never tasted the same. One day, I decided I was going to learn how to make Papaw's gravy and I did! Now, when I prepare the gravy, it is no big deal and I can "whip-it-up!"

It's important to remember throughout all of this though that the skill of cooking can take time, practice and patience. Because of this, it would be wise to start small at the beginning of your cooking adventures. Learn the additions and subtractions of cooking before you move onto algebra and calculus. You may want to begin with a list that I call: "I want to learn how to cook this." Begin to build your list slowly and increase it as you progress and feel more confident. In fact, let's do it together!

Right now, create a list of the following: two pork dishes (stuffed pork-chop, grilled pork-chop), three hamburger dishes (hamburgers, meat loaf and meat-balls), four chicken dishes (fried chicken, baked chicken, BBQ chicken, chicken and dumplings), and five vegetable dishes (mashed potatoes, baked potatoes, green beans, corn and broccoli). Eventually, you will feel comfortable to perhaps include three pasta dishes and maybe two homemade soups — throw in some corn bread and you are on a roll!

Many families love pizza and Tex-Mex nights. You will also want to discover two desserts you enjoy making. Lunches are easier because you only need to create a few quick and easy lunches with a simple salad recipe, as well as one or two homemade salad dressings. Finally, master one nice breakfast and you are a cook!

You may even want to celebrate by getting your very own chef's hat!

I have found that breakfast is a wonderfully easy meal to share with a friend. It's a great way to start any day and there are so many ways to prepare an egg. Scrambled eggs taste the best when cooked in butter with a little bit of milk, salt, pepper and a splash of water. Continuously stir as it is cooking, and you will cook a perfect scrambled egg! In our family, I am known for my waffles. I love my old waffle iron and it has served me well. Find what works for you and start making food memories today!

Serving up the Best

Most likely you've heard the saying: "The way to a man's heart is through his stomach." Well, I think there might be a little truth to the old adage. On one of my first dates with Terry, I cooked his favorite meal. I was not a very good cook when we first married, and for many years I wished that I could just hire someone to do all the cooking for me! But I have now learned the value of cookbooks and cooking shows. Even cooking shows can teach the most challenged person in the kitchen to cook with confidence.

Another helpful tip for expanding your cooking repertoire is to introduce yourself to a new recipe once a month. This will help to expand your cooking skills. And, even if you're single, nurture the spirit of hospitality in your home by serving your meal on your best china, lighting a candle and playing soft music.

Treasure Hunt

Now I would like to introduce you to what I call cooking treasures. Cooking treasures is like a treasure hunt for recipes. Start by calling a friend or family member and ask them what their favorite recipe is. If the recipe is challenging, ask them to come over and teach you how to prepare it. I learned a wonderful chicken enchilada and taco meat recipe this way. The secret for the ground taco meat is to cook it with a little, thinly sliced potato in the meat. What a difference this tip made! There are many cooking treasures all around you. You may not master the dish, but you will have so much fun trying. Make a cooking treasure date today!

Feeling Blue

Have you ever heard the term, "I'm singing the blues?" For example: "I'm feeling blue today," or, "I have a blue mood." Well, what if instead we captured the mood of hospitality and created the (positive) "blue-mood" of hospitality in our homes? Hospitality is not something we have to reserve only for times when guests are over. We can create an atmosphere all the time.

My dad got into trouble a lot for bringing strangers to our home. One couple he brought home needed to be put on a bus to get them to leave, while another family lived in one of my father's rent homes for one year, entirely free. I remember the look my mom would sometimes give my dad. One invited guest needed clothing and ended up abusing my dad's credit card.

However, of all the stories, the story of Mable is the best. My dad, as a young man, was Mabel's neighbor and she loved him like a son. Mabel loved on all the children in the neighborhood and always made sure none of the children were ever hungry.

Years later, my dad discovered that Mabel was in a mental hospital, so he went to visit her. He was shocked by the state he found her in. To this day I don't know how he did it, but he managed to sign her out of that hospital and brought her to our home. My dad placed her hospital bed in the middle of the living room, along with her portable toilet. My poor mom.

I was very young at the time, but I still remember Mable yelling through the night. She couldn't talk, and I was frightened by her; however, I watched as my dad restored her soul and spirit through love, care and time. She began to talk and eventually calmed down. My dad would hand-feed her and sing to her. She loved to hum the old rugged cross. Sadly, one day Mable's family came to our home and took her away from us. I cried like I did after the loss of my goat, Amy. Love with service changes people and it heals their hearts and souls, just like my dad's love and hospitality brought healing for Mabel.

The Value of Preparation

Good intentions must be accompanied with a good plan, and the best way to have a memorable dining experience is to plan ahead. I have discovered that the morning is the best time for me to plan the evening meal. It allows me to look at my day as a whole, so I can make time for a trip to the store if needed or prepare for food that may need to defrost. If you are like me, you will need to run to the store to grab what is fresh before coming home to cook it. Most meals will take only 30 minutes to prepare, once you are more familiar with cooking.

At this point, inviting the color blue into your home is easy! Simply invite family or friends over for dinner or brunch. Hospitality is the relationship between the guest and the host. This lost art in our society can only return if we invite hospitality to our table and into our homes.

Further, value the needs of your guests by being prepared. For example, if a friend calls you and needs to share her heart, either you could meet her at Starbucks to watch her cry into her cup of coffee or you could invite her into your home, to sit at your table.

Box soups have come a long way and they are easy to prepare in a short amount of time. For this reason, I always keep a box of roasted tomato soup in my pantry. I simply heat it up, add a little cheese on top, then I chop a few salad greens and mix a little olive oil with mustard and honey for a dressing. Just like that, you'll have a quick meal to heal the broken-hearted! There truly is nothing like warm soup to a hurting soul. Oh yes, be sure to serve it on your best china and you will be your friends hero!

I have a dear friend who, when I visit, never ceases to bring a smile to my face when she walks out of her kitchen with her tray of fruits, cheeses and crackers. Her tray is a delightful blessing and all it takes is a little preparation.

In Luke 22:10–13, we read the account of Jesus's last supper with his disciples. It was to be Jesus's last meal with the men who would be continuing His work and they needed a place to have their meal. Jesus instructed Peter, "As soon as you enter Jerusalem, a man carrying a pitcher of water will meet you. Follow him. At the house he enters, say to the owner, 'The Teacher asks: Where is the guest room where I can eat the Passover meal with my disciples?' He will take you upstairs to a large room that is already set up. That is where you should prepare our meal." They went off to the city and found everything just as Jesus had said, and they prepared the Passover meal there."

I think it's so amazing that the man of this house already had the room fully prepared and furnished. And, because he was prepared, he did not miss his encounter with Jesus. I wonder what that must have felt like to have Jesus and His disciples in his home for such an important occasion. The spirit of hospitality was already in his home and he was able to welcome in the Lamb of God.

When we invite guests into our home, it is important to remember that hospitality is more about the connection we are making with our visitors than it is about the "stuff" we use to decorate. Setting the stage for connection is simple; however, planning to impress someone is stressful.

Ina Gardner, the "Barefoot Contessa," says the best gift we can give someone is a home-cooked meal. By keeping your focus on the heart and the spirit of hospitality, you will enjoy your events much more.

Master of the Kitchen

Truly, the kitchen is the hub of hospitality. The essence of relational connection begins in our kitchens. So, in the same way we need to plan our events in order to anticipate the needs of our guests, we also need to prepare our kitchens so that they will be able to serve us and others.

Now it's time to talk kitchen design! The kitchen needs more attention to detail than any other room in the home. It's vital that you make the most of the space by keeping it orderly and functional. In addition, the kitchen is the best place to show off your favorite color because you want to create a space that you enjoy.

Personally, I love yellow, so my kitchen has pops of yellow with soft grays and whites. Most kitchens are designed in the popular triangle design, where the refrigerator, oven, stovetop and sink are in a triangle. This makes for the best flow, and flow in this space is what it's all about!

Counters should be clear with minimal décor—think active workspace. I like kitchens inspired by chef kitchens with open shelving, like restaurant kitchens. Even if your kitchen is small, try to have seating available which will encourage others to be able to sit and connect with you while you're cooking. I think that all-white dishware is the most practical choice and you can always replace them if one breaks. But feel free to get some with a little color too! My apron hangs inside my pantry door, and I always try to think functional and fabulous. My everyday dishes are china and I use crystal glassware daily. Why save the good stuff for once a year?

Coffee starts the day in our home, and Terry is the coffee king. We have a specific place for coffee in our kitchen and, if coffee starts your day like it does ours, you can too! I've designed master bathrooms around a coffee bar as well. Everything we need to host the family in the morning is right there at our fingertips. Our daughters, who no longer live at home, will even pop-in for a morning cup sometimes. Even coffee can be used to create connection and memories. Home is where the heart is, and the kitchen is the heart of the home, so we need to give home a heart beat!

Terry and I love having guests stay in our home and I love adding to their experience by placing fresh flowers in their room and bathroom. I also think it's a nice touch to provide something for them to read, air freshener, bubble bath, lotions and any other accessories that I feel may enhance their comfort. For my guest room I have chosen many calming colors—the linens are crisp and bright white, with pops of orange and yellow. I even have fresh water, nice towels, and a folding suitcase stand like a hotel would have.

Try and imagine yourself in the space as a guest. Do you feel relaxed and welcomed? Do you need to add a bedside book or a box of tissue? Try to preemptively meet the needs of your guest. By doing so you will be creating space for the spirit of hospitality!

Once, I listened to a sermon on Mary and Martha and the preacher asked us, "Are you a Mary or a Martha?" I squirmed a little in my seat because I knew that I was a Martha, always stressing over what to serve my guests. I would imagine that Mary was good at ordering takeout and Martha knew how to bake cheesy bread. (More about cheesy bread later.) The best news, however, is that we can be both! We can feed our guests, while also ministering to their hearts through hospitality. And blessing the food before each meal is a great place to start!

When we bless the meal that we are serving to our family members or guests, we are starting the meal with an attitude of gratitude. Terry knows the value of blessing the meal and he never feels in a rush to do so, but our little six-year-old granddaughter always asks if she can bless the meal. We thought this was so cute, until the other day when she explained to us "why" she wanted to bless the food: "Papaw prays too long!" Shortly after this, we were treating our grandson Mason to dinner for his tenth birthday and he wanted to bless the food. After blessing the food, he proudly looked up and said, "See! I did that in about five seconds!" Ok, so maybe they are not quite receiving the value of blessing the meal! But blessing the meal is a powerful way to invite hospitality into your dining experience and into your home.

Children and Hospitality

I remember the days when children were not served their food until after all the adults made their plates. The motto of that day was, "Children are to be seen and not heard." While we do not have those extremes today, I do believe that balance in this area would be helpful. With this in mind, I have trained my grandchildren that manners are needed at the table and, at the table, we "dine and don't whine."

I have trained my sweet little ones that the table is the place to learn communication and listening skills. One of our favorite dining, activities is to play the "thumbs-up, thumbs-down" game. This is a fun way for each child to share what the highlight was of their day, while also sharing what the low-point or thumbs-down was. Games like this create moments of connection around the table and can turn the simple act of eating dinner into a dining event. Moreover, the table becomes a place where each voice is heard, and we can listen to one another as we talk about our day.

My grandchildren also know that at my table every night is a "Food Adventure." The idea here is for everyone to try at least a bite or two of everything being served. Food adventures are even more successful when I allow the children to participate in the food preparations and the table setting. I brought my grandchildren into my kitchen experience when they were young, and I encourage you to do the same if you have children.

Another type of food adventure is eating outdoors. I have always felt that food tastes better when you are dining outside. Whatever the situation, by looking at it as an adventure, you will be better able to make space for family connection.

Unfortunately, I wasn't very good at getting my girls involved when they were little—perfectionism was my nemesis. Sadly, I had a "do it myself," attitude. While I am very thankful for the influence of women such as Martha Stewart and others in our society who show us a more excellent way of living, I do feel that there has also been a certain element of frustration as we strive for the mythical version of perfection. Perfectionism robs our joy and fun, causing us to compare ourselves and our events with others.

Tea Please

I always enjoy tea time with my precious granddaughters—even my energetic grandson wants to participate! I wish teatime was a tradition in our home like in the English culture, but sadly it is not. However, in regard to teatime, the plan is to always be ready. I enjoy keeping a variety of lovely teas and tea cookies in my pantry. I enjoy using my favorite teapot and teacups because they create such a fun feel to the occasion.

An elegant tea setting adds an emotional quality to your hospitality and helps to engage the senses. My little grandchildren always feel so special when we have tea time together. They enjoy drinking from my fine china teacups, while conversing with me like they are little adults. I will even allow them to invite their friends and to serve the tea. Oh, the memories we have made all while welcoming more hospitality into our home!

> The table becomes a place where each voice is heard, and we can listen to one another as we talk about our day.

Quick-nic

It has been my experience that some of the best memories are created when we leave perfectionism behind and embrace spontaneity. For me, spontaneity comes in the form of what I lovingly refer to as a "quick-nic." A "quick-nic" is a picnic that is done fast.

I have a basket prepared with plates, napkins, forks and a table cloth that I keep ready and available at all times (throw in a Frisbee or a ball to add a little game-time fun). When I am struck by the need to create a little outdoor fun with my grandchildren, I simply add grapes, cheese and chips, or any lunch items to my basket along with drinks and I immediately have a "fun-factor" for our day.

Another idea is to grab fast food on the way and put it in your "quick-nic" basket. Again, the focus here is not on the event, rather, it's about the connection you will be making with your loved ones. You may even enjoy surprising a friend with a "quick-nic!"

Recently, I took my grandchildren, along with my basket, to our town-center. It was a perfect December day and my sweet grandchildren were smiling from ear-to-ear, commenting that we were the only ones getting to have a picnic.

My precious grandchildren had a blast and the park was playing Christmas music, while the Texas sun was shining. You see, it isn't necessary to wait until the 4th of July to create an "outdoor" memory. Once we return home, I simply reload my basket for the next wave of spontaneity.

"Quick-nics" are a great way to create connection and memories. The preparation takes a few minutes, but the connections made will last forever.

Pause and Ponder

Take a short pause and go get your calendar. Create an appointment for a tea-party and "quick-nic," then let the fun begin!

Remember, like the perfectionist, I use to think that in order to have a picnic, I needed to fry chicken, make baked-beans, and whip-up potato salad with homemade brownies. Now, with a little wisdom under my belt, I realize that if I make the event hard it will most likely be costly and not as much fun, plus I will be less likely to do it.

Just think to yourself, "Let's have a fun adventure, and who cares!" How do you think I felt that day during the picnic after watching Santa visit the kids and singing Christmas songs with my four favorite little people? The answer is: balanced, relaxed and refreshed. And you can experience those feelings with your loved ones as well!

The Surprise

I remember one special event when stress was somewhat of an understatement. I have had very few surprise birthday parties in my life, but the ones I have had are memorable for very different reasons.

For my 18th birthday, dear friends of my parents, John and Lana, hosted a surprise party for me. John thought of a clever name for the party (which was a take on my own). He called the party a "Deb-utante Party!"

Yet my 30th birthday party was by far the most memorable, and not for the right reasons. My dear husband was not born with the planning gene; however, he was trying his best. I was known for my club sandwiches that I would layer with bread, cheese and two different meats. I would cut them into four triangles, garnish them with cherry tomatoes and pickles—displaying them on a tray.

My husband told me that we were going to his aunt's home and everyone wanted me to bring my sandwiches. I rushed about getting my little girls ready and my sandwiches done. I only had time to put curlers in my hair and I decided to take them out during the drive. Terry hurried me along and out the door I went—curlers and all, holding my lovely tray of sandwiches—only to discover that our parents were on my front porch! Surprise! My mom, who was holding the cake yelled, "Happy Birthday!" I had just made sandwiches for my own birthday party. To make the story even better, Terry forgot to invite any of my friends!

I want to share with you another birthday, to show you the value of adding emotion and meaning to your events. My sweet girls planned a fiftieth birthday party for me. They asked that everyone wear red (we had everyone wear pink for a baby shower once and everyone loved this fun idea). There were at least 30 of my closet friends in the room and I went around the room sharing with each of them how much their friendship added to my life.

Making the connection with your guest is key for inviting the spirit of hospitality into your home, or event. The color blue is the second most popular flag color, next to red, so wave your blue flag of hospitality today and begin making memories!

The Dinner Party

Do you know that blue is the best color to wear if you are making a television appearance? So, if blue is best for the camera, what should we wear to a dinner party? First, wear a plan, and then wear simplicity. The idea is to enjoy your guests and not to be overwhelmed before their arrival.

Again, planning is everything and the menu should be simple. Be sure to set the mood with soft music and candles. I love cloth napkins and placemats. For you, maybe setting the table the night before will help to save time, or placing your table-cloth, placemats, napkins and table decor into a basket you can easily access to set your table when it is time. This way everything will be in one place and will help to eliminate stress.

You can transform the look of your table simply by learning one or two napkin folds and adding fresh flowers in a lovely vase. To simplify the dinner party even more, you may choose to purchase a meal from a restaurant that is already prepared or buy a dessert, thus you won't have to cook at all. The event will be effortless, and the memories will be timeless. Host a dinner party soon and invite hospitality into your home!

I will never forget a dinner party I went to that was hosted by a dear friend. When we arrived, she made us feel welcome and, upon sitting at her table, I noticed she had covered her table with brown paper. She had written a beautiful quote about friendship on the paper and she wrote each of our names by our place setting. For the centerpiece, she wrapped brown twine around small pots of herbs. The aroma was amazing, and the effect was stunning. She prepared a simple pasta dish and the night was unforgettable. She truly had welcomed the spirit of hospitality in her home.

Yet if you cannot make friends with your kitchen or you feel that cooking is just not for you, there is no shame in being a takeout queen! Just make the emotional connection when you take it in. Serve it on your nicest china and create a dining experience!

Make a Plan

Make a list of the people you would like to invite to your home. Create a plan of how many dinner parties you would like to have in the next few months. The number of guests is up to you. I enjoy entertaining small groups of people, a couple to six guest works best for our home.

In your planning, choose what you will be serving and how you plan to make it memorable. Create the plan that is right for you and work it! Make hospitality connections, have guests bring a dish, or plan a progressive dinner party—salad at this house, soup at yours, then dessert at the next. Don't be afraid to color your life with many blue shades of hospitality!

Culinary Art

Like learning any art form, the process of learning to cook, and learning to create an atmosphere in your home of hospitality takes time.

Give yourself lots of grace as you are learning, and make sure to keep a good sense of humor with you at all times. During my "crash-course" of learning how to cook, I discovered a recipe for cheesy bread. I had no fear of baking, so I decided this was the perfect recipe for me. I loved cheese, so I more than doubled the amount of cheese that the recipe called for. I carefully followed the rest of the recipe and placed my bread in the oven.

The bread baked and baked and baked. No matter how long I left it in there, it was still not ready (gooey bread is not a good idea). It was 2:00 a.m. and my mom came downstairs where she found me sitting at the table with my head down and my eyes barely open. "What are you doing?" she asked. I sadly replied, "Baking bread." Mom told me she would finish baking my bread and she quickly sent me to bed. I was glad to go. Well, guess what—the bread was never done!

In the morning, we sliced and toasted the gooey mess and ate the whole thing: more cheese than dough! As you grow in the art of cooking, you may also get a repertoire of funny stories along the way.

Learning to create the "blue" environment of hospitality, including learning to cook, takes time. And, just like my father-in-law's gravy that I couldn't rush, we cannot rush the process. I have now learned that in order to make a good gravy you need to cook the flour slowly, and you must stir the mixture the entire time in order to achieve its perfect creamy and yummy taste.

In addition to time, having the right tools in the kitchen will also aid even the novice chef. I have learned to love a good chef's knife and I have a favorite cutting board. In the same way, it will take time for you to gather the right tools for your kitchen, and it will take time for you to create the right environment of hospitality.

Today, I truly enjoy connecting with my kitchen because I understand its value. I also appreciate taking the time needed to create an atmosphere of hospitality because I understand its value too.

Remember, you don't have to be a great chef to make meal times special and build meaningful connections. So, in the process of creating meals for those you love, don't forget to add the rainbow of health to your plate. The more colorful your plate is, the healthier your body will be. Red tomatoes, strawberries, orange carrots, yellow squash, lemons, green bean, leafy greens, blue berries, purple grapes and egg-plant are all great foods to add color with.

Be intentional about bringing "blue" into your home and making your meal a time for hospitality. Be encouraged that the rewards of cooking and connection with your kitchen are great and the memories you are creating there will bring heart to your home, lasting a lifetime.

INDIGO

Chapter Ten

TIME TO TRUST

"Yesterday's the history, tomorrow is a mystery, today is a gift of God, which is why we call it the present." –Bil Keane

The phone rang. I picked it up and heard the dreaded news that my sweet grandmother, Anna, had passed away. The nurse explained how, just before her passing, she sat straight-up in her bed and said, "I'm going home!" With these words, she departed.

I cried all the way to Ohio with my three little girls in the car. My grandmother and I shared a deep bond of love for 33 years. We enjoyed connecting over meals together, gardening and, of course, long talks. But what I loved most about Grandma Anna were the hugs she gave. Her hugs wrapped you in unconditional love and acceptance.

Her passing devastated my grandfather. I stayed the night with him and heard his cries and prayers deep into the night. I felt like my grandfather would never be able to recover from losing her. After some time had passed, however, I visited him, and I will never forget his words. He looked at me with such sincerity and said, "You can trust time to heal. Time makes it all better."

Time. Ephesians 5:16 exhorts us to make the most of our time, redeeming it. Time isn't material and it isn't one element. It can't be saved like money in the bank. It can only be spent. Benjamin Franklin wrote, "A stitch in time saves nine." He wasn't talking about sewing, rather, he was addressing the issue of how we can best use our time by spending every moment—every stitch—wisely.

Indigo

The dye for the color indigo was first discovered in England during the summer of 1289 from a plant. Indigo, not to be mistaken for blue, is rather framed in the color spectrum by blue and violet and, like time, it can get lost. I don't get many requests for the color indigo in my design business, yet, this color is so important to our rainbow.

Interestingly, the color indigo has one of the longest wavelengths in the visible color spectrum and, like time, indigo carries on. In fact, because indigo is a mixture of both blue and violet, it is a complex blend of introspection and insight—just like the passing of time. This is why indigo is the perfect color to symbolize time, as well as our need for it.

Time is essential for bringing color to our lives. And, just like trees need time to grow, our relationships, friendships, the training of our children, and personal progress all need time as well.

The Importance of Valuing Time

In this chapter, it is my desire that you would view time from an entirely new perspective. Like breathing in and breathing out, time just is. Yet so often we use it without giving it any thought or value. But I want to encourage you to engage with the time you've been given in a purposeful way.

We've all been given the same amount of time, yet, if you look around, you will notice the vastly different outcomes in the lives of individuals. Why is this? Because we all have a choice as to whether or not we will value or squander our time.

Personally, I have found that I must budget my time like I budget my income. King David prayed to God saying, "Teach us to number our days that we may get a heart of wisdom" Psalm 90:12 (ESV). You see, it's wisdom for us to number our days and for us to budget our time. We all have 168 hours, each week to spend and, because of this, it can take some "ponderings" and a great deal of "pause" to use each hour wisely.

We can "turn-up" the color in our lives and "turn-down" any dullness simply by trusting and valuing time. For instance, one way we can value our time is by intentionally creating habits in our lives that save time. Often, forming new, time-saving habits can be an effective way to put Ben Franklin's advice to work and make some little stitches in our present in order to save time for our future.

Keep in mind: habits take at least 21 days to form, so as we embark upon this journey of indigo, it's important to give yourself grace and understand valuing time takes time! Take for example an issue as simple as time spent trying to find your keys every day: without a thoughtful plan, this can be a sad waste of time. But if you were to formulate a system of putting your keys in the same place whenever you arrive home, you will then be able to save time in your time budget.

How many times have you found yourself rushing out the door, only to realize you didn't place your keys in the right spot? You'll then need to spend perhaps ten stressful minutes running around the house looking for them. There go your time-ticks!

Personally, I am guilty of needing to get one thing or another from my car late at night. Because of this, I usually place the keys in my robe pocket. Even so, I have started to value my time anew. The result is that I now return my keys to the same place and time is saved in my time bank.

Stop Signs

Another example where a stitch of time may be saved is when we set stop signs on toxic relationships. We all know someone who may be living their life through others, or their mission is to change someone else's life choices. Or, perhaps it's someone who calls you several times a day so that you can save them from their latest catastrophe!

Whatever the case may be, toxic relationships are just that— toxic. You can pray for these individuals and live a godly life that is an example, but please know that you cannot make someone happy. Happiness comes from within, not without, and only God can bring true change and contentment. Be aware of relationships that are only robbing you of your valuable time. You will not only save time in the long run, you'll also have a lot more peace of mind!

Those who know me well, know my love of art and how I love to paint. Nonetheless, painting is a very time-consuming hobby. For this reason, I have chosen not to spend my time-ticks on art and painting during this season of my life.

Right now, I have my precious grandbabies who are so young and who adore me. I know the day may come when they will outgrow hanging out with Grammie, so I am saying "no" to some things so I can invest in what God has placed in my life during this season. Still, I do plan to spend time on my art during a future season of my life. I'm just waiting for

One way we can value our time is by intentionally creating habits in our lives that save time.

when my grandchildren are older. Again, time is like money in the bank: it is limited, and we must be wise as to how we spend it and how we save it!

Pause and Ponder

Okay, you know what to do! How do you presently view your time? What are you not spending time on that you would like to? (Note: the answer may be more than one or two items.) Taking time right now to reflect is essential, as we will refer to this journal entry later on.

Think about your time-budget: you have 168 hours each week, and hopefully you are spending at least eight hours a night sleeping. Furthermore, work is most likely 20-50 hours a week, in addition to the drive time. How much time do you spend on your quiet-time, church, shopping, meals, self-care, housekeeping, volunteering, watching a favorite television show, hobbies, date night etc.? Subtract these hours from your bank of 168 and evaluate how many time-ticks you have remaining.

I would like to ask you to keep a time journal for approximately two weeks. Trust me on this. The time journal will give you a more informed idea of how you are spending your time. You may find that you are not as busy as you think, or you may see that you need to let go of a few things in order to better balance your time budget.

Remember, the goal is to use your time-ticks on your biggest priorities first. In addition, also ask God to show you if there are people in your life who may be toxic, and you need to love from afar. You will be able to connect with your family to a greater degree as you unplug from toxic relationships. Personally, I have a couple people that I love dearly, but from afar.

Taking Control of Your Time

My family traveled a lot when I was young. Because of this, it wasn't uncommon in my childhood home to only have 30-minutes notice when preparing for a trip. And I never knew where we were going!

Once, my father decided to take my two brothers on a spontaneous fishing trip to Canada. Dad wanted to "live-off the land," so they took no provisions. After being dropped off at a cabin in the middle of nowhere, they discovered that the fish were not so easy to catch. Thankfully, they discovered a box of macaroni and cheese along with some potatoes that someone had left behind. They were much slimmer upon their return, but my brothers will never forget their last-minute adventure—two boats and the lake to themselves.

My mom and dad always loved to travel and have family adventures, so getting ready in a flash was important in our family. My dad sold motor homes, so traveling across country was common for us. I can still get ready in 30 minutes flat to this day, but this is because I have learned to care about time. I have learned to take control of my time and use it productively, so it serves me well. And by managing your time wisely, you will be able to add value to your life.

Stephen Covey once said, "You define what is important to you by what you dedicate your time to."[1] In order for us to put those words into practice, we must determine the difference between what is important vs. urgent in our lives.

For instance, a call from my husband or children is important, while a call from one of my clients is urgent. Items that are important have greater significance and value in our lives, while items that are urgent, though pressing, don't necessarily take first priority. Both the urgent and the important possess meaning, but one adds far more color to my life.

Take a moment and read your last "Pause and Ponder" answer. What are you not doing right now due to lack of time? Don't put off goals and dreams for the things that are urgent but not important.

While taking control of our time is essential, there is another side of time that can be slightly more challenging and it's knowing when to give-up control of our time to someone else.

Personally, I am married to "Mr. Right-on-time." Plus, Terry is always the life of the party. He would easily enjoy being the last to leave every event (but I won't let him). He loves people and has never met a stranger. His favorite conversation starter is, "How 'bout them Cowboys!" You would be surprised to see how many responses he gets to this question—no matter what country he is in! He is always able to get people talking and make them feel truly special. I have had to learn, however, with his talents and his need to connect with people, to let go of the control of time and realize that time is not always my own. You see, it's important to know when to wisely give up control of your time and enjoy the "just being" moments.

Inch-by-inch

Have you ever noticed how much a person can get done in 15 minutes? John Bytheway wrote, "Inch by inch, life is a cinch, but yard by yard life is hard." Similarly, life 15 minutes at a time is sublime, but day by un-designed day is lost time. If we give value to each 15-minute segment, we will build hours of great value and substance.

Keeping this in mind, I have learned to view my time in sets of 15 minutes. If I do something for 15 minutes four times, I know I have just spent 1 hour of my time-ticks. Similarly, if I went out to eat 10 times in a month and spent $40 each time, I would know I have just spent $400 of my real money.

Time, like money, is real. And when it is gone, it's gone. Yes, you can get much accomplished in 15 minutes, however, there is more value in the un-rushed life.

By learning to take life in small increments, we can be more productive with our time. And, when we are better time-stewards, it can actually make the pace of our life feel less rushed.

Now, you may be thinking you need to fill every moment, but it's important to plan your time so you can still have moments when you let go of time. To do this, we are going to learn how to design our time in the same way we design our homes. It feels natural to think about defining our style and identifying how we wish to add color to our lives, and in the same way it should be natural to think about designing our time and calendars.

Personally, I like lists and I plan ahead. I like to set appointments and arriving early is a high value of mine. Seven is the number of the colors in the rainbow and the number of completion. I try to keep my lists at seven "to-do's" for each day. For me, appointments for a given day may be worth two or three spots on my list. I may need to design and select fabrics for window treatments or pick up art. All of these are accounted for on my list. I limit myself to working with seven clients or less at a given time. Once, I had 33 clients at the same time and it was overwhelming!

My life is much more peaceful now that I understand the importance of setting limits and boundaries on my time. I have learned how to manage my time better through experience.

A Colorful Balance

I also believe in scheduling what I call "Nesting Days." Nesting day does not mean you are preparing your home for a new baby;

though, it does mean you are preparing for new life—a new life full of color!

For me, a nesting day is a day I design to be all about the home and a time I can address my home and personal to-do list. There are no rules for nesting day, it's just like playing house. I can take my time and focus on a home project during a nesting day, I can take a break and call a friend for encouragement, or I can plan a design idea. Sometimes, my nesting days feel like a mini stay-cation!

In addition to nesting days, I have pajama days, where I treat myself to a home facial while drinking tea and enjoying a good book or movie. Do I often have days like these? No, these days are not on my weekly calendar, however, I do book these on my calendar so that I can be sure to enjoy my "Designer Days."

You might not be able to spend an entire day as a "Designer Day," but you may be able to schedule for yourself a late morning or afternoon. You might even be able to take an evening to experience a time you have designed. Find what works for you and schedule it on your calendar.

Relationships are a high priority in my life and keep me feeling energized and centered, thus I always have lunch with a friend on my calendar. Once I have finished one lunch date, I quickly book the next friend.

The simple act of having lunch with a friend, even if it's only once a month, builds relational equity over time. I also feel it's important to have family activities scheduled on my calendar. Again, have the prospective that you are making your priorities, priority. Spending my time-ticks on making connections is a high value for me.

In the 1950's, a beauty consultant to movie stars advised his clients to spend one full day each week in bed resting. And, their food was to be served on a tray. I don't know about you, but I think this sounds nice! We may not have the luxury to spend an entire day in bed, but spending a morning in bed should be planned into your calendar a few times a year.

Not only should you design a day for rest and nesting, but you should also design days for fun! When you budget your time-ticks for days that are relaxing and enjoyable, then the days you must spend your time bank on work or other tasks, won't feel as burdensome.

Life is more colorful and flows much better when your calendar is balanced, and you have something to look forward to and hope for. If you hear yourself saying, "I don't have time," that is a sign you need to take a closer look at your time bank balance.

Super Mom

Scheduling "Designer Days" is important for everyone, but it is especially valuable for busy moms (though many moms may feel like time is working against them!).

I remember when I was a mom of young children I thought I had to do it all. Every morning I donned my superwoman cape. At the time, I was friends with another young mother who was

> "He that can take rest is greater than he that can take cities."
> -Benjamin Franklin

bright and bubbly. To me, this friend always appeared happy and calm. I, on the other hand, always felt stressed and was busy overbooking myself. My bubbly friend would place her daughter in a weekly Mother's Day Out program, while I was busy trying to do it all myself. I felt that since these sweet daughters were given to me, I alone should care for them.

Eventually, I did place Tessa in a one-day-a-week Mother's Day Out program and I became a different person! I was now the calm and peaceful mom. But for you, maybe consider trading out childcare with another mom one day a week if funds are limited right now. A few hours of self-time deposited into your time bank will do wonders!

Pause and Ponder

What would a day without limits look like for you? How would you spend a day, if you had nothing but time? Dream big! Would you tackle your to-do list, visit with a friend, take a bubble-bath, go for a long walk or have a home-spa day? Maybe you would love a day walking around town with your honey or having a fun-factor day with your kids or a niece. Perhaps you would enjoy having a day of prayer, fasting and devotions.

With your list made, grab your calendar and design days just for you. Schedule moments of "me time," making even small parts of your day a get-a-way. This will ensure you are making time to add color to your life. Call a friend and book a lunch or coffee. Fill that calendar with color! It is too easy for the color indigo to get lost in the rainbow or the color spectrum; in the same way it is too easy for your dreams to get lost in the busyness of life. Add indigo to your calendar—you will be glad you did!

Top Time Thieves

In our modern world, there are distinct time thieves: smart phones, social media, television, and individuals who don't value our time. I have seen too many people watching their phones, waiting for a comment regarding their previous post, while their important time-ticks are ticking away: time thieves.

Further, television is like the black-hole of time, once you enter, you may never come out! I don't believe the news is so important that we need to know what is happening every minute. Remember what Dr. Leaf said? Our brains cannot multitask activities, thus they cannot multitask cerebral input. We can turn up the indigo in our lives by turning down media's volume.

Once upon a time, I was a seller of Mary Kay cosmetics. I was 19 and, in addition to learning many valuable lessons, I was having a lot of fun. I must say that the highlight for me was meeting Mary Kay in person. She treated everyone with great value and, when you left her presence, you felt as though you were the only sales woman she had.

Mary Kay knew the value of time and she kindly taught us her tips. If you were on the phone with a wordy client, one trick was to look at the doorbell and say, "There's the doorbell! I have to go!" There are some individuals who have no value for your time and you must learn to say, "No," or, "I have to go now." I no longer have a doorbell that I can see, but I use this same principle in different ways. Find what works for you and guard against the time thieves!

> ***"And the evening and the morning were the first day. And God called the light day, and the darkness he called Night; and the evening and the morning were the first day,' and there was evening and there was morning, one Day."***
> ***Genesis 1:5***

The start of your day sets the tone for success. Because of this, it's important to developing your morning routine so you walk out your door fully charged. Yet mornings can be a struggle. Getting beds made, kids out the door, and having quiet time can be a great challenge. But seeing our day from a new view point may help.

The evening has everything to do with the morning, and if the Father's plan was that evening started His creation, he started from the end. When we pause to think about the effects evenings have on our mornings, then going to bed at a proper hour, having a bedtime routine, and planning for the day ahead becomes more valuable. Like designing a room, keep in mind, the art that will be displayed or pillow you love. Starting the project with the end in mind makes a difference.

Time Marches On

In the movie, *Steel Magnolias*, the character, Truvy, says, "Honey, time marches on, and eventually you realize it is marching across your face!" Claire Belcher later states, "You know you would be a much more contented, pleasant person if you would find ways to occupy your time."

Have you ever noticed how time is unapologetically bold? And, while indigo is a peaceful color, it is bold as well. Because of this, we must become more bold regarding our time.

Do you hear the heart-beat of time? Time is so valuable and has the capacity to make enormous deposits into our relationships if we spend it wisely. So, be assertive. Personally, I enjoy starting my day slowly and finishing it fast. This may sound crazy, but it works for me. I am an early riser, which allows me a generous amount of time in the morning to have quiet time and coffee with my husband. There is no rush as I get ready for my day.

You may enjoy having a workout and going over your plan for the day. My work is never complete; one client's list may grow, while yet another client is waiting on fabrics or painters. Yet, regardless, I try to book my work days with limits and self-value.

There was a season of my life when I didn't understand the value of time and I over exhausted myself—arriving home completely spent, with little to give my family. But now, I manage my time-ticks. Further, I used to skip lunch, but as part of valuing time and myself, I book a lunch hour in my day, making sure to relax and stop all calls. My time management strategies help me to be more focused during my work hours because I know that I have also planned time for rest and end my day at 5:00 p.m. or 6:00 p.m.

I have learned to communicate with my clients that I have personal stop-signs regarding after hour texts and emails. I let them know that I wrap up my day at 6:00 p.m. These stop-signs help to communicate the value that I have for time. I greatly value my clients, but I must also value their time and mine.

Remember, no one is going to value your time except you, so

manage it well. Again, managing your time in the same way you manage your money will add value to your life. But adding many splashes of indigo to your life canvas takes balance and planning.

Pause and Ponder

One time, I called a dear friend to tell her my plan to treat her to an art retreat. She replied, "No, I really don't want to spend my time that way." I love that I have friends who are comfortable telling me exactly what they think regarding a matter.

Are you able to tell a dear friend, "no"? When it comes to how you spend your time, do you find it difficult placing stop signs for yourself? Do you fear losing that friend if you were honest with them and expressed the true value of how you would like to spend your time? Have a discussion with your friends regarding this topic. Discover how they might be thinking or feeling—you may be surprised!

Is there someone or something that is robbing your time? How can you stop the stealing? Go look in your mirror and practice saying, "No!" This may be a first for you. I remember saying "no" to someone for the first time and I thought the world was going to stop! But you know what? The world didn't stop and yours won't either! Maybe you just need to tell your "Superwoman" alter-ego "no" and say "yes" to a life full of indigo's beauty.

Time to Be CEO

My daughters and I love to people watch. One time, we were at a theater where they serve food as you watch your movie. A troop of Boy Scouts happened to also be enjoying the movie and I couldn't help but notice what a frenzy the troop mom was in. She frantically ran around explaining in detail how the snacks were on the way and how they would be delivered and so on. She was wearing old, dirty sweats, no makeup and her hair was a messy "I don't care" style.

I pondered her value of time—her value of self. It is a noble act to give time away to your child, however, I wondered how her son would feel if he had a mom who cared about balancing her self-care with him. "What did her son think of her," I pondered. Yes, you can enjoy your child's extra-curricular activities, but love for others isn't about losing yourself in the process. I know this through first-hand experience.

I was the mom who had to give the best school party. My motto was "perfection." One of the end-of-school year parities that I planned is talked about to this day with prizes galore, food, rides and a climbing wall. But do you know by the end of the day I could hardly even walk? It took me two days to recover from that event.

You see, a good CEO is in charge, but also allows others to shine as well. A CEO plans *with* the team, giving others encouragement. CEO's are proactive in problem solving, preparations, and time management.

When I was a young mom, getting three little girls out the door was not an easy task. With this in mind, I always told my girls our leaving time, not our arrival time. I planned extra time for mishaps like the lost shoe, the spilt milk, or the meltdown. I was the CEO of our time, so I planned accordingly.

You cannot "go with the flow" as the CEO or overseer of your life. I am not implying that God is not ultimately the one who is in charge of your life; nonetheless, we need to value His divine time. No one is going to pack that diaper bag for you or give you extra time to handle that last-minute meltdown.

Proverbs 22:3 says, "A prudent person sees trouble coming and ducks; a simpleton walks in blindly and is clobbered" (MSG). Have you ever felt "clobbered" by life due to a lack of time management?

Now, you may be thinking, "Deb, you have no idea how out of control my life is!" Let me encourage you. You may feel overwhelmed right now, but by caring about your time, you will be able to bring some peace and order to your day.

CEO's are great planners. I know a few CEO's and they aren't last-minute ladies—they even get a good night's sleep! You see, good CEO's understand that procrastination is their enemy so they "call the shots" in their lives. They are empowered to give commands to those who are under their command in order to get the job done.

If your family has never had a CEO, they may be a little disoriented at first, but take charge of your home. Take inventory of the needs and pulse of your home, then formulate a plan that will help to create peace in your life as you color in the lines of indigo.

Your time is valuable. You are valuable. Trust that God will give you the time you need as you submit your plans to Him. "Commit everything you do to the Lord; trust Him and He will help you" (Psalm 37:5, NLT).

God wants you to trust Him with your time and each day. Yes, you are the CEO, but you don't have to do it alone. He wants to help you. All you need to do is just ask.

Trusting God

He cares about every detail of our lives. For some people, trusting is a difficult concept, yet God says, "You can trust me." You see, trust is the belief that something or someone is reliable, good, and honest. And God is GOOD! So, trust that He will make all things in your life beautiful in its time. Trust that God, who began a good work in you, will be faithful to complete it. Trust that God has a future and a hope for you.

The inability to trust others is crippling, but the inability to trust God is devastating. Oh, what color God wants to bring to our lives if we would simply trust Him! Believe in God's loving power He has poured upon your life and let Him have the final say in your day—it will make all the difference.

Trusting God with our time happens when we allow God to be the Master of our "to-dos" because He cares about every detail of our lives. However, like any relationship, trust takes time. So, if you find it hard for you to trust God, give Him time—get to know Him like you would a friend. I did, and I was surprised by the love that He lavished on me. And He has the same love for you.

When you begin to trust God, you will also experience less fear. Fear, as it relates to time, has many forms. Some people may fear they will not have enough time to do what is on their heart. Some may fear that time will expire too soon. While others may fear that they will not have provision in the future.

My precious Mamaw was very conservative, but she had to be. While she was but a young bride of 19 with a precious two-week-old baby, she instantly became a widow when her husband was killed in a dump truck accident. This experience affected her in such a way that she didn't part with things easily.

Mamaw had to place my mom in the care of a sweet pastor and his wife just to go back to school. She later married my sweet Papaw, Harvey. Later in life, after Papaw died, my Mamaw waited 20 years before parting with any of his belongings. It was Christmas time when she decided it was time to pass on Papaw's socks to my brother. The socks were so old that my brother's foot went right through them. This may sound like a funny story, but it's important not to be afraid regarding time. Some things in our lives have expired just like those socks, but we need to be willing to let them go and move on.

Do you have out of date relationships, out of date ideas that you might be desperately clinging to out of fear? Don't put it off any longer! Time expires. Live your time to the fullest!

Time-ticks—we all have the same amount, but what we do with them will make all the difference. You will add value and color to your life when you begin to value your time by creating systems that save time, adding structure to your life, and living in the moment. God truly makes all things beautiful in their time.

Pause and Ponder

So, here we are at the end of our beautiful color indigo. Do you feel God's color wrapping around you? I do. His rainbow surrounds us with His promises. But in order for us to fully receive all that He has for us, we have to trust Him.

In this final "Pause and Ponder" for indigo, I want you to find a quiet space. Meditate on what God is speaking to you right now. He always wants to talk to us—we just have to listen. So, listen. What is the Holy Spirit saying to you right now? Write it down. Are there any areas in your life where it's hard for you to trust God?

Ask God to show you ways to fully trust in His love for you. As His daughter, He desires for you to live life well, so see His gift of time as a blessing each day. God is able to work all things and all "time" work together for His and our good.

Isaiah 43:2 says, "When you pass through the waters, I will be with you; and when you pass through the rivers, they will not sweep over you. When you walk through the fire, you will not be burned; the flames will not set you ablaze." And King David declared in Psalm 56:3, "When I am afraid, I put my trust in you."

Today, no matter what you are going through, no matter what your time-ticks are filled with, trust God. Commit your time anew to Him and watch what He can do!

VIOLET

Chapter Eleven

GOOD GRACIOUS GIRL

"I do not understand the mystery of grace; only that it meets us where we are and does not leave us where it found us." -Anne Lamott

I was the tallest girl in my elementary class—chubby with fuzzy brown hair. And, while I was a creative and spunky eight-year-old, I had a tender heart. Most days at recess, I could be found by the swings with my three best friends: Cindy, Rebecca and Judy.

My friend, Cindy, was blonde and had pierced-ears. She and I both liked Sam Miller and, one day, we even had a fight about him and I pulled out one of her earrings! Judy, however, was the complete opposite. She had a quiet nature and, because her parents were divorced, was being raised by her g randmother. Judy was the only child I knew from a divorced home, and we all felt sad for her. My friend Rebecca had dark brown hair that was cut in a perfect bob with straight bangs. I felt sad for her too, but for different reasons. Rebecca's family didn't celebrate Christmas, nor was she allowed to attend the school Christmas party. I thought this would be a terrible fate, until one day I was able to attend a party at her home. I realized her family still had celebrations—just different from any I had known. Her mother gave Judy and me a dreidel during the celebration and explained how they have a very long Jewish celebration called Hanukah. After that, I didn't feel sorry for Rebecca again!

On our school playground was also a group of African American girls who always seemed to be in motion: cart-wheels, flips and giggles. I often noticed one girl named Esther, whose smile and bright eyes were so full of life. She always seemed to be wearing a beautiful pressed dress in a solid color and, at the end of every dark braid, was a perfectly matching bow. My favorite was her yellow dress, it had a full flowing skirt with a bow neatly tied in the back. She would often catch my eye and smile while we waved at each other, but we never played together.

One rainy day we were to have recess inside. The cafeteria tables were moved against the wall in order for us to have room to play. My friend Judy was sick, while Rebecca was out of town and Cindy had remained to help the teacher. There I was—alone. Suddenly, Esther appeared and, taking my hand, told me she wanted to show me something. I sat mesmerized as she sang "Flowers on the Wall" by the Statler Brothers.

"Counting flowers on the wall, that don't bother me at all.
Playing Solitaire till dawn, with a deck of fifty-one.
Smoking cigarettes and watching Captain Kangaroo."

Her body was moving like nothing I had ever seen before, hips swinging from side to side. She would then turn quickly and point her toe in the air. It was delightful! At that moment, I was transformed, and I was her biggest fan. Finally, she pulled me to my feet and tried to teach me the dance. I could sing the song, but I could not copy her moves.

We laughed and giggled until our sides hurt. I wish I could say that after that day we were the best of friends, however, as the rain faded so did the moment we shared. The next day, life resumed in the usual fashion as I returned to the swing set with my gang and she returned to her friends in the corner of the playground.

I will never forget the last time I saw Esther. My dad was selling my horse, Silver, to her family so off we went to her home. It was a Sunday and, as my dad was talking to her parents, Esther, in all white with bows gleaming in her hair, beamed me a smile while waving enthusiastically.

At that moment, shame filled my heart, and I looked down. I had never known such guilt before. It wasn't the guilt that I had experienced after doing something wrong—it was from a much deeper place. This guilt and shame would remain, galvanizing my little heart.

After that day I would always think of Esther whenever I heard, "Flowers on the Wall," or when I would try to dance in my room. I was haunted by the fact that I had not returned the friendship and love she had shared with me. I didn't have God-given grace at the time to do the right thing, and I was never able to express to Esther how much I appreciated the special friendship she offered to me that rainy day.

Grace is the power that heals guilt and shame. As an adult woman, remembering this childhood incident, I realize how important it is to allow grace to govern our lives. Grace is an effective weapon against shame and guilt. The shame that I felt regarding my lack of friendship for Esther was quickly accompanied by pain. However, God's grace is able to heal the shame that I experienced: banishing my pain. But not only does grace heal, it also allows us to embrace who and how God truly made us. While grace means smoothness, elegance, and courteous, good will, it also means God's unmerited favor. Grace truly is amazing, and it is represented in the final color of our rainbow: violet.

The Color of Grace

I believe violet to truly be one of the loveliest colors in the rainbow. Violet, a softer version of purple, denotes royalty, majesty, and kingship. In my design profession, I have had several requests for this color, and not for the usual little girl's room, but for clients who love the richness of violet and purple (which pairs best with gold and hints of copper).

The color of violet embodies a sense of mystery with its royal qualities and was once considered the royal color of ancient Caesars. In the same way violet is the crowning glory of our rainbow, we need to allow ourselves to be crowned with grace. Grace and violet, both possess a gentle power that enables us to act with goodness and courteousness.

Grace for Who You Are

Were you born self-confident? Like many, I was not. However, as I studied the Bible, I realized that I am a daughter of the King of Kings. 1 Peter 2:9 says, "But you are a chosen people, a royal priesthood, a holy nation, God's special possession, that you may declare the praises of him who called you out of darkness into his wonderful light" (NIV).

When referring to us, God's daughters, Psalm 45:13 says, "All glorious is the princess within her chamber; her gown is interwoven with gold." As the bride of Christ, we receive power through grace to live above sin and shame. The psalmist declares, "Let the King be enthralled by your beauty" Psalm 45:11 (NIV).

You may be blessed with a family in which your parents instilled you with a healthy sense of self-value and the belief you are the King's daughter. Most of us, however, experienced broken families and seemingly endless ugly stages where grace was nowhere in sight and violet was merely a color on the spectrum—not a way of life.

Maybe you feel like you are still in an ugly stage. My cute friend (with the perfect blonde hair) during my adolescent years, once told me, "Your feet are so big—you're too tall, and your hair is so fuzzy! Don't you know they have straighteners for that or you could just cut it?" I was not happy that day with the package God had put me in, and I didn't have the grace I needed to process her comments.

I still remember my first pimple. I was young, and our class picture was the next day. We were busy remodeling our farmhouse and I happened to notice some sand paper. I know what you are thinking: sand paper and skin are not a good combination.

Well, when my mom received our class photo, she couldn't help but notice that all of the children were looking forward with big smiles, while her loving daughter was turned completely sideways. I had turned quickly to the side just as the photographer had said, "One, two, and three!" I desperately wanted to hide the quarter-size scab on my forehead. I was embarrassed and doubted that God could be enthralled with my beauty.

In the 70's, I wanted to look just like Cher—door-knob hipbones, with long, straight, shiny hair. To this day, we have family photos where I used so many chemicals that my hair looked like orange straw! During this season too, I was not excited about the package that God had put me in. Yet, as I have allowed grace into my life, I have been able to fully embrace the way God made me.

Jeremiah 1:5 says: "Before I formed you in the womb I knew you, before you were born I set you apart" (NIV). Psalm 119:73 and Psalm 139:13 say, "Your hands made me and formed me...For you created my inmost being; you knit me together in my mother's womb" (NIV).

My friend, God does not make mistakes! How delighted are you with the package God has placed you in? Are you able to say like the prophet Zephaniah: "For the Lord your God is living among you? He is a mighty savior. He will take delight in you with gladness. With his love, he will calm all your fears. He will rejoice over you with joyful songs . . . you will be disgraced no more" Zephaniah 3:17-18b (NLT).

If you are not confident in how God has made you, the answer is this: grace. By knowing the One who made you in the image of His grace, you will become more aware of how valuable you truly are. Your loveliness is timeless, and it isn't based on the latest look of the day, the way you style your hair, or how you wear your makeup. True grace and loveliness come from being in the presence of God and knowing Him.

Personally, it wasn't always easy for me to know who I was in Christ. I remember one day during my quiet time I came upon Psalm 46:10: "Be still and know that I am God" (NIV).

In our stillness, we are able to seek God and know Him personally. It's in God's presence, we will be changed as we see Jesus more clearly and study His word. 2 Corinthians 3:6, 16–18 says, "[It is He] who has qualified us [making us to be fit and worthy and sufficient] as ministers and dispensers of a new covenant [of salvation through Christ] . . . But whenever a person turns [in repentance] to the Lord, the veil is stripped off and taken away. Now the Lord is the Spirit, and where the Spirit of the Lord is, there is liberty (emancipation from bondage, freedom). And all of us, as with unveiled face, [because we] continued to behold [in the Word of God] as in a mirror the glory of the Lord, are constantly being transfigured into His very own image in ever increasing splendor and from one degree of glory to another; [for this comes] from the Lord [Who is] the Spirit" (AMP).

True grace and loveliness come from being in the presence of God and knowing Him.

When you begin to see yourself the way God sees you, experiencing His grace, self-assurance and confidence will begin to rise from deep within you—transforming you by Christ's love.

Makeup and a Broken Leg

It was my sixth-grade year when I received the honor of playing the witch in our school play, *The Wizard of OZ*. Our teacher, Miss Smith, who had never been married, was overseeing the play. Now, Miss Smith always wore too much red lipstick. It was fascinating to watch her liberally applying it at the front of the class. She applied it several times throughout the day, always dabbing her bright red lips with a tissue. To make it more interesting, her cheeks matched her lips.

On the night of the play, Miss Smith thought it would be a marvelous idea for us to wear makeup for the Play. I couldn't have agreed more, so I eagerly ran to get permission from my mom who was sitting with her friend. "Mom, can I wear makeup for the play?" I asked breathlessly. With a voice of shock and contempt, my mother's friend said, "You go tell that teacher that you are a good girl and good girls do not wear makeup!"

Well, I'm sure you can guess that I hated my mom's friend after that. I knew my mom didn't wear makeup, but I felt that if wearing makeup made me a bad girl, then I wanted to be a bad girl! What was I to do when there seemed to be so many conflicting routes for goodness sake? Grace and goodness seemed unobtainable to my adolescent mind and I was determined to have my graceless way.

If you haven't realized it by now, let me tell you, growing-up I had a few issues following rules. I loved Betsy McCall paper dolls and one time I decided to tear them out of the magazine from our local library! As always, my sin found me out, and I was soon whisked off to the library, so I could deliver my full confession. I was instructed to tell the librarian what I had done and that I was sorry for stealing the paper dolls from the magazine.

The library had a large window and my parents decided I needed to repent alone, so they watched me from the window. As I went inside the library, I managed to tuck the paper dolls inside a library book. My parents watched as I approached the front desk. I told the librarian, I was returning the book for my mom because she had broken her leg. As I said this, she and I both turned and looked sadly at my parents through the glass. I never told my parents what really happened. The guilt I felt from that day left quickly; however, the shame—not so fast. But I have learned that through God's grace we can leave all our shame and guilt at the foot of the cross, no matter how big or how small.

Grace or Pride

Have you ever tried to mix oil with water? The two do not mix, and grace and pride are the same way. Try as you might to whip them together, time will separate them. There is chaos and confusion when pride and grace try to share a space. You must let go of pride before grace can truly flourish. Grace desires to make space for your life, while pride wants to bring constriction. Grace will tell you to ask for help, while pride says, "I don't need anyone." Grace loves light, forcing shame to flee, while pride tries to hide shame and guilt in the dark. And while grace is empowering, pride causes us to pretend we are fine when truly we are suffering. Yet receiving grace doesn't have to be hard. It simply starts with a yielded heart, one that is willing to lay aside old ways of thinking and live submitted to grace.

Do you find it difficult sometimes letting go of old ways of thinking? Do you cling to perceptions of yourself that may be outdated? I remember one time when I was determined to cling to my own ideas of how things should be as a small girl. My Mamaw was sending Papaw to town, and I wanted to go!

Papaw Harvey drove a truck at the time that had running boards on the side. I decided, after being told, "No," that I would ride to town on the passenger-side running board. But at the last minute, my Mamaw decided to go to town with Papaw. As she walked around the truck to get in, there I was hanging on with all my might. I had decided that I was going to town and nothing was going to stop me.

Looking back, I realize that if my Mamaw had not discovered me hanging onto the side of that truck, most likely, I would have bounced off and died on the side of the road that day. This story seems funny now, but it's a picture of how we sometimes hang onto wrong choices or beliefs in our lives. There have been seasons in my life when I was so convinced in my wrong choice that I went a long way down the wrong path before I came to my senses. Now I see that if I had simply stopped, paused, and taken the time to ask God for His grace to empower me, I would have been saved much humiliation and wasted time. I am committed to making space for grace in my life because of memories like these. I know first-hand what life looks like without God's grace and it is not a soft violet color. In the same way that we readily make room in our homes for beauty, we must also make space in our hearts for the beauty of grace.

Let It Go

Now, you may be wondering, "How do I make space for grace

in my life?" I think in many cases the answer is quite simple: let go. A favorite song of my granddaughters is "Let it Go" from the Disney movie *Frozen*. I love hearing them sing it again and again, and the lyrics teach a powerful lesson through those simple words: let it go. But in the same way we must be willing to let go of old ways of thinking or perceptions, we must also be ready to let go of old seasons to fully make room for grace in our lives.

I helped pioneer the widow's ministry in my local church. For three years, I worked hard and took great care in planning all the events. While it was difficult for me to understand their loss, I greatly desired to serve them and see them flourish. During this time, it was on my heart to pray that one of the widows from the ministry would feel led to take on the leadership of the group. The day came when the group began to take flight with new vision, as I began to transition out of the ministry. It was hard for me at first to let go of such a meaningful season when it was just beginning to get its wings. Nonetheless, I knew that my season had ended, and I needed to let go.

Letting go isn't always easy, even when you know it's God's plan. In the same way that we are saved through grace—not our own power—we can also, through grace, find the right balance for our lives. The background color of our life canvas should be violet, covered in goodness and grace. Violet is such a sweet color and complements the other colors, letting them stand out boldly. In the same way, grace is gentle, so fully receive and let it flow through your heart and mind.

Pause and Ponder

Let's pause and ponder, so get that cup of tea or coffee (try using your favorite mug or tea cup to add value to the occasion). Do you wrestle with doubts, shame, or guilt, wondering if you are a good girl? Like me clinging onto my Papaw's truck, are you clinging on to old ideas of who you are and who you are yet to become? Is there a season or a ministry in your life that you are determined to make work, even though you know it isn't the plan God has graced you with right now?

In reading through the colors of the rainbow, you may have felt like you don't measure up, that somehow, you've missed the mark or let your family down, but it's my desire that you would experience violet (grace) for yourself and your home.

Through my journey, I have discovered that God can encircle my life canvas with His rainbow of grace, and He can do it for you. God is not a respecter of persons and He wants to meet you right where you are. Grace comes from Him alone; we cannot manufacture it. Grace is God's beauty flowing through us and we simply have to receive it. With this in mind, be still and listen for the voice of your heavenly Father saying, "My good girl, receive My favor. You do measure up!"

When you release all shame and guilt to God, you will be able to view those spaces filled with the color violet and grace. God's grace empowers us to let go of guilt and shame and to trust that He doesn't make mistakes.

The Violet Dress

Receiving grace is like receiving a gift but, like any gift, grace must first be received and stewarded. As a young girl, my father was diligent and hard working. His efforts provided my family with plenty and he loved taking me shopping every Easter for a special new dress. I looked forward to this tradition year after year.

One year, however, I noticed a young girl in our church who was poor, and I asked my dad if I could buy a new dress for her instead. I was excited as I carefully selected a soft violet dress that would complement her blue eyes. On Easter Sunday, I arranged her hair, and she wore her brand-new Easter dress. Though I was wearing my old dress, I was also wearing a great degree of pride as we entered the church service together. She looked so lovely. I felt I had changed her life forever. However, two weeks later, my heart sank as I observed the large stain down the front of the soft violet dress that was now wrinkled from lack of care.

I had graced someone with a gift that was precious, but they didn't receive it with the same spirit and value. In the same way, God has given you a gift, a gift of grace that will take your heart and make it new. God's grace enables you to be victorious and brings you goodness. The question is, how will you receive it?

In order to fully receive God's grace and become the woman He wants you to be, you must let go of the lie that says, "You are not good enough." God wants to grace you with powerful freedom to live out the plan He has for you. So, plug into the rich power of grace, and value yourself to fully receive it.

Esther is my favorite woman in the Bible because she showed courage in the face of adversity. Yes, the king saw her attractive outward appearance, but I believe he saw something even greater—the beauty of her spirit. As a woman of poise, I believe Esther must have had an elegant and graceful bearing about herself. She understood how to receive and steward grace and, because of this, she was able to rescue the entire Jewish people from a sure death.

I sometimes wonder if she felt "less than other girls" because she was orphaned. I imagine she didn't feel very beautiful. She most likely didn't notice, as she was busily taking care of Mordecai, the goodness and loveliness that graced her countenance. Maybe she was one of those girls who didn't need makeup, who simply looked fabulous by pulling her hair up, no matter what she was wearing.

No matter what she looked like though, she still needed grace and confidence in order to fulfill God's plan for her life, which was going before the king to make a request. Had Esther not stewarded the grace she had been given, the Jews would have been killed. But because she received grace and was confident in God's plan for her life, she was not only herself blessed, but she also dispensed it to others. We are called to do the same, to be "Esther's" in our generation and to our families.

Esther must have also been a woman of poise. The definition of poise is "a graceful and elegant bearing in a person, with balance and self-control." Truly, poise is having beauty and dignity from the inside out. With so many women vying for the king's favor, she won his heart. Now, our society values beauty from the outside. But grace, goodness and poise start on the inside. A woman who knows her true worth will be filled with grace and good works.

Like Esther, we are called to arise and let grace, balance our lives with true elegance and self-control. A poised woman dispenses grace to others just like Esther did.

Designer Diva

There was one season in my life when grace was not natural for me. I was busily building my design business and, yes, I was a design diva—I know, shocking. I was obsessed with my work and I would often enter the workroom, where the fabricator would be busy at her tasks, demanding that a window treatment be reworked because the seam was not straight. Or I would get upset if the design didn't match my complicated drawing. What's more, I did this with no grace or thought for how I was making my workroom attendant feel.

One day, I received a letter from the attendant (who received a third of her income from me) informing me that she would no longer fabricate my designs. WHAT! Me!! "How could you not want to work for me?" I thought as I read her letter. She went on to say, in her letter, that I made her extremely stressed and her stomach would be in knots every time I entered the work room. She explained that after praying about it, she felt that it was God's will I no longer be in her life.

She prayed about me not being in her life! I could not believe it! What a "hit on my heart" this was for me. I definitely needed to "pause" after reading her letter. I needed her talent, but because I had not extended grace to her or allowed myself to be graced by her friendship, I was without the skills she possessed. I begged and pleaded to no avail.

Looking back on this time, I am grateful to her for that letter. It forced me to re-evaluate not only the way I receive grace, but also how I may or may not be extending it to others. Now, in my business, I first receive and extend grace through friendship and courteousness before I ask about a design job or project.

Through grace, God changed my heart and I was able to let go of the shame and guilt that I felt that day. But it was difficult at first. I began to ask God to show me the grace He had for me. I asked Him to help me see myself through His eyes. "What did God think about me and my selfish ways?" I wondered.

For the next two weeks, during my prayer time, I began to hear the word: "surprise." I had no idea what "surprise" meant. Was God saying He was surprised I was still here? I had no idea.

One day, I needed to purchase a new cell phone and my daughter offered to select a song for my ring-tone. When she asked me what I would like, I said, "Surprise me." The next day, when my phone rang, I was greeted with James Blunt's song, "You're Beautiful." I couldn't believe it! God was singing right to my heart, and I was soaking up His grace.

Later that same day, I was attending my last appointment at 7:30 p.m. (these were the days I struggled to trust God to bless His plan for me) and my client walked up to me and said, "I have a surprise for you!" She then held out two diamond rings and said, "Pick one." As I looked at the rings I thought, "Which ring do you want me to have, Father?" I was able to pick the ring that fit perfectly. As I drove home that night, I was overcome by the grace of God on my life.

Over time, I have realized that the power of grace I receive flows through me, affecting others around me. We cannot give away something that we do not have. To be a violet vessel full of grace, empty out the diva heart and humbly receive the repair of grace.

Freedom and Grace

Kintsugi is a centuries old Japanese method of repairing pottery by filling the cracks with gold. Some call this method *the art of precious scars* because it embraces something broken and makes it more beautiful and of greater value.

In the same way, I believe that freedom and grace walk hand in hand. We must have freedom to grace others, freedom to forgive those who have caused us pain, and freedom to grace ourselves when we fall short. What does living fully in grace look like for you? My *grace* motto is this: "Allow God to replace my superwoman cape with wings. Ask daily for help with each task I face. Relax knowing, He has my back, and view the colorful masterpiece of my life canvas through His grace-filled eyes."

So, did you have a week when you didn't spend time having fun with the kids? A day when you threw grace out the window, as you threw hamburgers into the back of the car? Did you lose your keys or forget your daughter's purple shirt for the field day? Or, perhaps your boss over loaded your week, causing the rainbow of colors in your life to become dull and out of focus.

If yes, now is the time that you need grace for you! Color this part of your life in gently with violet and stand tall knowing that God is able to lavish you with grace. Pause and ask yourself if you could have made better choices, and grace yourself for the next day, knowing His mercies are new every morning. Great is His faithfulness!

Pause and Ponder

So, here we are at our final "Pause and ponder" for this chapter. Becoming a gracious woman of violet means learning how to receive grace, while also knowing how to give it away. There is beauty in grace and women who possess it stand-out. A woman of grace knows that God has her back! Did you know that when viewing the rainbow your back must be to the sun? Well, in the same way, as you view the rainbow of your life, the Son, Jesus Christ, has your back!

As we pause to add violet to our lives, quiet your heart and snuggle-up in your favorite spot and, oh yes, grab that cup of tea or coffee. How is grace expressed in your life? Do you struggle with feeling unworthy or undeserving of the King's favor and love? In order to have the life that God designed for you, receive His gift of grace and goodness.

Now, what would you like to request from the King of Kings today? Write down your answer and today's date. Like Queen Esther, go before your heavenly Father with the power of grace at your back and make your request known. Do you need to feel His love surround you or His favor in an issue today? Do you need help in managing your life? Do you need Him to show you the next step in the journey?

Be still and let these words wash over you: You are altogether lovely, clothed in violet and arrayed in His splendor. You are loved. You are violet!

Chapter Twelve

GRAY SKIES

"There is an appointed time for everything.
And there is a time for every event under heaven"
-Ecclesiastes 3:1-8, NASB

I feel like everything in this book has led to this chapter. I have found there is no joy in color, unless I have first experienced the gray days. We all have areas in our lives where there is no color. I have gray areas in my life and they used to define me. But now, I have allowed the Light of God to shine through them and, consequently, these gray areas have healed. This is not to say I will never experience another gray day; however, I now know that my faith will see me through—coloring in my gray with God's light: God's color.

My parents would often sing a song titled, "Thank You for the Valley I Walked Through Today," by Dotti Rambo. The song goes:

> Thank you for the valley I walked through today. The darker the valley the more I learn to pray. I found you where the lilies are blooming by the way. And I thank you for the valley I walked through today. Thank you for every hill I climb for every time the sun didn't shine. Thank you for every lonely night I prayed until I knew everything was all right. And I thank you for the valley I walk through today. Life can't be all sunshine, or the flowers would die. The rivers would be desserts all barren and dry. Life can't be all blessing or there would be no need to pray. So, I thank you for the valley I walk through today.[1]

Just like King Solomon wrote that there is a time for every season under heaven, there is also a time for the valleys in our lives and for the days that are gray. In the Sermon on the Mount, Jesus declared: "He gives his sunlight to both the evil and the good, and he sends rain on the just and the unjust alike" (Matthew 5:45,

NLT).

It is hard to understand sometimes why difficult times come and why we experience the gray in our lives, but we can trust God that He will make all things beautiful in their time.

Difficult Memories

What I'm about to share with you is very personal. But I share it with you because I want to encourage you that no matter how difficult the memories of your past may be, God still has an amazing plan for your life. He can use the bad times—the gray days—for your good and His glory. It may still be hard, but I can assure you He is faithful, and you can trust Him.

Now, the gray days came very early for me when I was only a young girl of eight. To this day, I still have memories that are covered in gray—a hazy kind of gray that hinders me from seeing the past clearly. Often, when a child experiences a trauma, their undeveloped mind records the memories in a confusing and broken manner, which is true of my childhood experiences.

I attended church regularly as an eight-year-old, going to camp meetings and Sunday school. There was an elderly pastor in our church who was always kind to me, and he would come and find me during every church event. I looked forward to seeing him because he would play with my ponytail and tell me I was pretty.

My mom and I were very close, and I would always sit with her—many times we would even dress alike. I think my mom didn't fully trust this elderly pastor. One evening after church once everyone had left, my mom got distracted as she was talking with a friend who was in need in the back of the church. The elderly pastor appeared in my pew and sat next to me.

I looked into his face that contained that same warm smile with grandfatherly eyes. Without saying a word, he took my hand and touched himself inappropriately. My little confused mind knew that this was wrong, but I didn't know what to do. And, to this day, I cannot tell you how this experience ended: did my mom walk up, or did he walk away? The memory is gray.

More gray came into my life through the abuse I experienced from one of my dad's cousins who lived and worked on our farm for a short time. I wish now that I had told someone so that his other victims would have been spared. I had never been instructed when I was young regarding "right" and "wrong" touching, or that I should tell someone if I was being touched.

These situations were so confusing for me to process at such an impressionable age, and they wove their way into the fiber of my being to such a degree that they became a part of me. Subsequently, I wasn't able to identify that I had been abused until I was almost 30. It wasn't until my forties that I realized how desperately I needed help addressing the gray areas in my life and the damage my heart had received. I realized that I needed to find a safe place to share the burdens of my heart—to let the light shine. I needed to get all the gray in my life out of the darkness of shame. Through Christian counseling, I was shown how to let God shine through the gray. That's when I began to experience true freedom.

Letting the Light In

Forgiving those who have hurt us in our past isn't easy—especially when it has become intertwined within your soul. And it's a process that cannot be taken lightly. Personally, I had never had the thought or desire to forgive the men who had abused me. In fact, I had suppressed their actions against me—keeping them locked in the dark places of my heart. But once I decided to open my heart to God's amazing light, I was shocked at the amount of gray that was hidden there.

Yet there are still other gray days Terry and I have journeyed through. Early in our marriage, we desired a family. I tried to have a baby, however, after an ectopic pregnancy and two miscarriages discouragement settled upon us like a gray cloud with no rain.

One day, a friend of my fathers called and shared with me that there was an 18-month-old baby girl named, Mary Beth, who had been abandoned by her mother. Terry and I were informed we could adopt her—she would be ours to love and care for.

I had toys and clothes prepared for her arrival. Mary Beth was delightful and quickly became the light of our lives. She began to call us "mommy" and "daddy" and loved meeting daddy at the door—greeting him with her chubby-cheeked smile. She slept in our bed and was understandably very clingy, due to her mother leaving her. She never wanted anyone but me holding her. She was mine and I was hers.

No matter how difficult the memories of your past may be, God still has an amazing plan for your life.

One day, however, her mom returned, and I was informed that I had to place her on a van that was Florida bound. I tried not to cry as I packed her little suitcase with all her precious things that I had purchased for her with such anticipation and hope. She was crying, and I knew that in some way she felt like I was abandoning her as well. The individuals who were taking her from me had to pull her off me because she wouldn't let go. I tried not to cry as I waved goodbye, watching that sweet baby wail and cry as the van pulled away. I watched until I could no longer see the van.

Once back inside my house, I went to the bathroom and fell to the floor, curling up into a ball—I thought I would never be able to rise again. Later, the people who had taken Mary Beth away returned to speak with Terry. They asked him if we wanted to take Mary Beth in with us again. Terry told them no. I never knew this conversation had taken place until years later. I didn't keep up with Mary Beth or inquire as to how her life turned out. I did receive a photo of her when she turned 18, but I couldn't look at it for long. By that time, God had blessed my life with three precious girls of my own. The gray days were long gone, replaced with many colors. Joy for me came in the morning.

The Rainy Day

All of us have a story. We all have tales filled with gray memories cocooned in haze and colorless days. Yet somehow, God is able to make a rainbow out of our pain and bring His color into our darkness.

A dear girl I know, Tiffany Adams, experienced one of the saddest days I know of. Tiffany grew up playing with my girls. She was delightful and full of joy and life. She always loved singing at the top of her lungs into her hairbrush, and now serves on our church's worship team. My heart swells every time I see her standing in front of the congregation so tall and beautiful—singing praises to the Lord.

I was blessed to watch her mature from a young girl into the beautiful woman she is today. She married a wonderful young man and the two of them have built a precious life together: buying their first home, her husband started a successful business, Tiffany serves on the worship team, and both are constant in faith, hope, and love.

They always desired children, but were unable to become pregnant. For eight long years, they waited and prayed. Finally, the day came when they discovered they were expecting. Furthermore, they were expecting twins: a boy and a girl! Their lives were complete. But as time progressed, Tiffany went into labor too early. The doctors informed the anxious couple that due to complications regarding the baby boy's health, his chances of survival were low.

Family and friends prayed and prayed for the babies to be healthy and for both to survive. The day that Bryce and Clara were born was covered with both great joy and greater sorrow. Bryce was so pure and perfect, his parents lavishing his short time on earth with love and affection. After only 18 hours, his precious life on this earth ended. However, his little sister, Clara, was thriving.

I attended little Bryce's funeral with great sorrow and heaviness in my heart. I couldn't even imagine what the pastor was going to say during such a grievous occasion, yet his words will stay with me forever. He said, "A thousand years is as a day and a day is as a thousand years to the Lord. What a difference a day makes." As they placed their little son in his grave and sent balloons with goodbyes into the gray, cloudy sky, the clouds parted, and the sun appeared with a rainbow surrounding it. In their grayest day, God's color was still shining through their storm.

I was soon blessed with the opportunity to design the nursery for baby Clara. The idea was my daughter Taniea's, and she worked much harder than I did. Once we were done, Clara's little nursery was cheerful, calm and peaceful. I felt that Tiffany and Erik needed a room that would be a place of joy, grief and reflection. Their nursery had a very sweet spirit and was so inviting. Yes, what a difference a day makes.

Erik and Tiffany are now blessed with two little girls and a son, and I have watched Tiffany's bright smile return as she has allowed God to shine through her gray with His healing light.

From Gray to Light

"Nothing weighs on us as heavily as a secret."
-Jean de La Fontaine

Secrets can hurt families. Why? Because secrets are gray. Yet sadly, many families have secrets—areas shrouded in darkness. Secrets have the mysterious ability of being able to hold captive its owner. And the fear of keeping the secret from coming to light can be paralyzing. I am truly shocked at the number of dubious individuals among us, the posers pretending to be someone on social media that they are not, while they live a life of complete deceit. Yes, many times the truth does hurt, however, the truth will set us free.

John 3:21 says, "But he who practices truth [who does what is right] comes out into the light; so that his works may be plainly shown to be what they are—wrought with God [divinely prompted, done with God's help, in dependence upon Him]" (AMP). God desires that we would always walk in the light, and that our secrets would come out of the darkness into His marvelous light.

One of my grayest days as a child came upon the discovery of my parent's secret. My cousin Tony and I were sitting in my corn crib, having a mini-adult conversation about divorce. My friend Judy's parents were divorced, and she was being raised by her grandmother. My friend's situation was very upsetting to my nine-year-old mind (there were fewer divorces in those days).

Cousin Tony looked at me and said, "Well your parents were divorced!" I yelled back, "Oh no they weren't! You're a liar!" Immediately, I ran away yelling as I searched for my mom. When I found her, with panting breath, I said, "Mom, Tony is lying. He said that you and dad were divorced!"

My mom was standing in our farmhouse kitchen and she closed her eyes, dropping her chin to her chest. Sadness filled the room as she tried to form her words. "Tony's right," she said simply. "I have been trying to come up with a way to tell you. But for you to fully understand I will have to start at the beginning." As my mom wove her tale together for me, gray crept further into the recesses of my heart and mind.

At the age of 19, my dad, Tim, was serving as a jet mechanic in the air force. My mom, who was 15, was the youth leader at her church. She had decided to take the youth group to a church rally in Victoria, Texas. During the rally, my dad arrived with his girlfriend, Barbara. My dad didn't have a car and, after the service, some of the youth group piled into Barbara's car to go for ice-cream. Dad was behind the wheel as my mom was getting in.

Now, her mom (my grandmother) had just purchased a brand new 1957 Buick. I don't know if my dad was just wanting to drive that new car or if he had something else on his mind, but as my mom, Billie Janette, climbed in, my dad asked, "Are you going to ride in this old car when you can go in that brand-new Buick?" Mom jumped out of the car very offended and asked, "So who wants to ride with me?" My dad tossed Barbara the keys and said, "I do!"

And he did! They were not one to take their time courting and they had a beautiful wedding. Unfortunately, gray days came soon after because of their immaturity, which ultimately led to their divorce.

My Father was a very good-looking man. In fact, he looked like Elvis, and any girl would have swooned for him. And my mom was beautiful. She had the 1950's look of the day: long, dark, wavy hair and blue eyes with full eyebrows. Together, they were a good-looking couple.

I came along quickly and, since my parents had divorced, my dad didn't see me until I was two weeks old. I was the child of a 16-year-old, single Mom during this time. It took three years, but my dad eventually grew-up a little bit and came to visit my mom and me.

We were living in Houston, Texas at the time and Dad took Mom out for lunch. My parents couldn't eat a bite during lunch. Their love was still there, and it took them both by surprise. Tim then asked Billie to trust him to come back for us and he left. My mom didn't hear a word from him for a month, but, true to his word, he drove to Houston one day and picked us up. They remarried and off we went to Washington, D.C. where they celebrated their honeymoon with three-year-old me in tow!

Pause and Ponder

Do you remember the old black and white televisions? When I think of gray, I think of what it must have been like for people whose only experience had been a monochromatic picture. Then, suddenly, the TV becomes colorful and they see everything anew—full of light and brilliance. Can you imagine what a thrill that must have been to turn on the television and see color, when all you had ever known was black and white? Well, in the same way, God wants to take your gray—those days that may be shrouded in haze—and He wants to shine His glorious light into all of those dark places. All you have to do is tune in and let Him shine.

So, grab your journal and find a comfy place. Do you have your tea or coffee? Ask yourself: Do you have a gray day or days? How does it make you feel to think about God shining His light into the darkness of your gray? How can you allow God to start replacing your gray with color?

For many, Christ-focused counseling, freedom ministry or just talking with a friend may help. The simple act of bringing your gray into the light is so powerful. The sun cannot produce a rainbow if it's covered by clouds. This is why we must let the Son break though our cloud.

By God's grace you will be able to take one step of faith at a time, relinquishing your dark days to His healing light. Uncovering the gray in our lives is like turning on a color television for the first time—what a thrill! However, there will be times when the journey will be hard and challenging, but it is so worth it. My poor mom, standing in the kitchen that day, was so shackled with shame and fear, but today my parents have been married over 60 years (we don't subtract the tough years).

This process of letting the light shine upon your gray areas will take great courage. So, I want to encourage you to be brave and know that God is for you, not against you. The Lord declares, "Do not fear, for I am with you; do not be dismayed, for I am your God. I will strengthen you and help you; I will uphold you with my righteous right hand" Isaiah 41:10 (NIV). You can be brave!

Chapter Thirteen

I MADE THE RAINBOW

As I cried out to God in prayer early one morning, my heart felt like it would melt within me. Tears began to flow down my face. I was deeply troubled over the suffering that a beloved family member was experiencing. My heart was heavy, and my prayers felt heavier—desperate. Instead of a victorious prayer of faith, my prayers felt like dark rain clouds heralding a storm.

As I lifted up my eyes to heaven, I pleaded with God to move in the situation, and in that moment, something happened. Like a cool breeze on a hot summer day, a peaceful calm washed over me—cooling me—then God whispered, "I made the rainbow." Suddenly, I sat up straight and repeated the words aloud, "I made the rainbow." My spirit stirred, and I responded back to God, "Why yes! You did!" In that declaration, hope entered my heart. I realized that if God made the rainbow, who am I to doubt He will not redeem the mess that my family member was in by giving them beauty for ashes and bringing them joy in the morning? My heavenly Father knows I am a visual person and the image of the rainbow was just the encouragement my heart needed. I needed to believe that God had this situation in His hands.

I was so moved by God's gentle answer to me that "He made the rainbow," I began to research and learn everything I could regarding the rainbow and how Almighty God had created it. What I discovered left me speechless. Did you know that the rainbow is made from the colors in the sun? By viewing sunlight through a prism, you discover that the light from the sun consists of red, orange, yellow, green, blue, indigo, and violet. And, if you mix all these colors together, you get white—which is what the sun looks like to the visible eye. To us, the sun just looks like a bright light, but it is actually where the colors of the rainbow come from.

Author, Donald Ahrens, in *Meteorology Today* describes it this way, "A rainbow is one of the most spectacular light shows observed on earth."[1] The rainbow truly is God's artwork—His masterful centerpiece that captivates every person, no matter their age. It's amazing to me how the colors of the rainbow are always in the same order and no two rainbows are alike. Even more fascinating is that each person sees a rainbow differently because our eyes (being unique) catch the colors and view them through droplets of water through our perspective and position.

Did you know that the rainbow is a circle, but the earth gets in the way, making it look like an arch, with the sky under the bow bluer than the sky above? And have you noticed how rainbows are mostly seen after a rain storm? Perhaps it is God's way of saying He sees us, and it's His way of reminding us of His promises.

God: Full of Color and Light

As I was studying God's perfect work of art, I was reminded of how our God is full of bright color and light. 1 John 1:5 says, "God is light, and in Him there is no darkness at all" (NASB). The prophet Ezekiel also declares in Ezekiel 1:28, "As the appearance of the rainbow in the clouds on a rainy day, so was the appearance of the surrounding radiance, such was the appearance of the likeness of the glory of the LORD and when I saw it, I fell on my face and heard a voice speaking." Habakkuk 3:4 says, "His radiance is like the sunlight; He has rays flashing from His hand."

Truly, God is full of bright color and character just like Ezekiel prophesied. And when we allow God to shine through us—even the gray and dark places—we will produce the same red (hope), orange (deliberate character), yellow (faith), green (peace), blue (hospitality), indigo (trust), and violet (grace) that comes from Him and from His promise of the rainbow.

The first rainbow can be found in Genesis and is proof of God's covenant with Noah and the generations to come. Genesis 9:13-17 says,

> I have placed my rainbow in the clouds. It is the sign of my covenant with you and with all the earth. When I send clouds over the earth, the rainbow will appear in the clouds, and I will

remember my covenant with you and with all living creatures. Never again will the floodwaters destroy all life. When I see the rainbow in the clouds, I will remember the eternal covenant between God and every living creature on earth. Then God said to Noah, "Yes, this rainbow is the sign of the covenant I am confirming with all the creatures on earth" (NLT).

I can't comprehend what it must have been like for Noah and his family, knowing that every person on the earth had died and they alone had been spared. How did Noah feel about God's gift of the covenant rainbow? I can imagine he might have felt relieved. But think about it, every time you see a rainbow, God is seeing the same rainbow and He remembers His promise to us—His covenant—that "as long as the earth endures, seedtime and harvest, cold and heat, summer and winter, day and night will never cease" Genesis 8:22 (NLT).

The rainbow, which has been used as a display for baby nurseries, a symbol of right, and claimed by many organizations as a trademark, is actually created by God as a gift for all mankind. The rainbow is a covenant to me and to you that symbolizes what God is able to complete and add to our lives.

Jesus declared, "You're here to be light, bringing out the God-colors in the world" Matthew 5:14 (MSG). God takes the storms, the gray places, and yes, even your destructive messes, and makes them beautiful. When we allow God to fill our lives with His light and color, we will be like a prism to the world around us, reflecting the glorious rainbow-beauty of God.

Pause and Ponder

Take some time and just reflect on God. Take note of the areas His color and character are not shining through in your life. This question is very personal, so allow yourself a safe place to reflect and honestly answer. We started out with the lesson of how to color, outline and define the areas of our lives where color is needed. So now, looking back over your journey, how is your life canvas? Can you see it more clearly? Are the colors shining brighter in your life today than they were yesterday?

I would like to share with you one last story. My grandpa Roark loved to race and when he joined the army he could outrun most everyone. He was a very competitive man and, even as a coal miner, he was always the second in productivity at the plant (his father was first). Many mornings on the farm he would race me down the lane to the bus stop. There were 40 years between us and, even though I had long legs and he would give me a head start, he would still always win. I was always determined though that I was going to beat him.

"I have fought the good fight, I have finished the race, I have kept the faith"
2 Timothy 4:7 (NIV)

One day, as I was running with the wind in my face and my hopes set high, I realized that I was gaining on him! I continued to gain on him until I passed him right at the end of the lane. I climbed on the bus and couldn't think of anything else all day except my victory. Later that day, I bounced off the bus and all the way up the lane, ready to declare my win. I couldn't wait to find Grandpa and rub in my victory. I checked the barns and looked in the fields, yet I couldn't find Pops. Finally, I decided to go and ask Grandma where Pops was. After finding her, she said, "Oh honey, Grandpa is in bed with the flu!" Imagine my surprise in discovering the truth behind my victory!

Living life isn't about coming in first or winning. The important thing is to show up and fully participate. So, let your light shine and let your home and your heart be filled with many colors as you rise and run your race. You can do it! I know you can!

NOTES

Chapter 8

1. Stephen Covey, 7 Habits of Highly Effective People, (New York: Simon and Schuster, 1989).
2. Brady Boyd, Addicted to Busy (Colorado Springs, David C. Cook, 2014).
3. Caroline Leaf, Switch On Your Brain: The Key to Peak Happiness (Grand Rapids, Baker Books, 2013).
4. Ronny Hinson, He pilots my ship (Dayspring Music, Songs Of Calvary Music, 1972).
5. Jan Greenwood, Women at War (Gateway Create Publishing, 2015).
6. Brené Brown, The Gifts of Imperfection (Center City, Hazelden, 2010).

Chapter 10

1. Stephen Covey, 7 Habits of Highly Effective People, (New York: Simon and Schuster, 1989).

Chapter 12

1. Dottie Rambo, "Thank You for the Valley I Walked Through Today," (Brentwood-Benson Music Publishing, Inc.).

Chapter 13

1. Donald Ahrens, Meteorology Today (Cengage Learning, 2012).

CPSIA information can be obtained
at www.ICGtesting.com
Printed in the USA
LVHW081110160119
604042LV00001B/1/P

9 780578 425702